School by Design

A Field Guide to Transforming Learning, Culture and Place

Anne Knock PhD

Published in 2025 by Amba Press, Melbourne, Australia
www.ambapress.com.au

© Anne Knock 2025

All rights reserved. No part of this book may be reproduced or transmitted in any form or by any means, electronic or mechanical, including photocopying, recording or by any information storage and retrieval system, without prior permission in writing from the publisher.

Cover design: Tess McCabe
Internal design: Amba Press
Editor: Andrew Campbell

ISBN: 9781923403284 (pbk)
ISBN: 9781923403291 (ebk)

A catalogue record for this book is available from the National Library of Australia.

School by Design

For Soren and Rory

May your education be a journey
of inspiration, curiosity, creativity, and fun.
Go boldly. Make a difference.

Contents

About the Author — 1
Acknowledgments — 3
Preface — 5

Part 1: Foundations for Change — 13

Introduction — 15
1 From Classrooms to Learning Ecosystems — 23
2 Leadership as a Catalyst — 34
3 *Samepageness:* Building Alignment and Trust — 47
4 Agentic Learning Design — 56
5 The Power of Place: Rethinking Learning Spaces — 65

Part 2: The Playbook — 77

6 From Theory to Action — 79
7 Transforming Leaders: Laying the Foundation — 90
    Tool 1: *Looking Back Across Generations* — 97
    Tool 2: *The Leadership Charter* — 100
    Tool 3: *The One, The Few, The Many* — 102
    Tool 4: *Decision-Making and Action-Taking* — 104
    Tool 5: *Three Horizons Thinking* — 107
    Tool 6: *Impact Map* — 110
    The Elements Unpacked — 113
8 Learner Experience: Why We Exist — 114
    Tool 7: *Empathy Map* — 116
    Tool 8: *Journey Map* — 120
    Tool 9: *Pulse Check: Learner Experience* — 123
9 Professional Culture: How We Work — 125
    Tool 10: *Team Agreement* — 127
    Tool 11: *Agentic Learning Design* — 130
    Tool 12: *Pulse Check: Professional Culture* — 134

10	Management and Systems: How We Organise	137
	Tool 13: Regenerative Ecocycle	*140*
	Tool 14: Breaking Down Silos	*145*
	Tool 15: 1-2-4-All: Purposeful Meetings	*147*
	Tool 16: What? So What? Now What?	*148*
	Tool 17: Pulse Check: Management and Systems	*151*
11	Places, Spaces, and Resources: What We Create	154
	Tool 18: Amplifying Spatial Literacy	*159*
	Tool 19: Spatial Design Principles	*162*
	Tool 20: Affordances A-Z	*165*
	Tool 21: Designing for Future Learner Experience	*168*
	Tool 22: Pulse Check: Places, Spaces, and Resources	*171*

Final Word: It Starts with Trust		173
Appendix 1	Setting the Scene – Café or Classroom	177
Appendix 2	Café Design Principles Explained	179
Appendix 3	Spatial and Pedagogical Typologies	180
Appendix 4	Bubble Drawings	182
Appendix 5	A-Z Affordance Cards	184
References		185

About the Author

Dr Anne Knock is a strategic designer with a passion for helping schools navigate complexity. She has had a career in education spanning decades in teaching, leadership, school transformation, and professional learning. Anne works with schools and architects to align vision, culture, and the physical environment. Her expertise lies in guiding strategic change through vision alignment, fostering professional cultures, and supporting educators to reimagine their practices and environments for lasting impact.

Anne's work is deeply informed by her extensive experience in the education sector and her PhD research at the University of Melbourne. Her thesis explored how teachers successfully and sustainably transition into innovative learning environments within the context of complexity theory. Since 2010, she has led professional study tours across Australia, New Zealand, and internationally. Anne is a keynote speaker, workshop facilitator, and contributor to industry forums. Her mission is to help people thrive in a complex and evolving landscape.

Beyond her professional life, Anne remains in touch with the practice of teaching through her husband, Bill, who keeps her connected to the everyday realities of school life as a learning support teacher. She is the proud mother of two adult sons and grandmother to two energetic grandsons, who remind her why the future of education matters so deeply. A lover of the outdoors, Anne finds renewal in cycling, bushwalking, and other adventures in nature, and brings that same spirit of curiosity and exploration into her work and writing.

Acknowledgments

This book stands on the shoulders of so many who have shaped my thinking and practice over decades in education. To the students I have taught and learned alongside, and to the countless teachers and principals I have worked with in schools across diverse contexts, thank you for contributing to the rich tapestry of ideas and experiences that inform this work. Your openness, curiosity, and commitment to an education for the future of children and young people have been a constant source of inspiration.

In particular, I wish to acknowledge the pioneering team at SCIL: Dr Stephen Harris, Steve Collis, Michael Harris, and Michael Appleford. Working with such a creative group of educators was a joyful, unpredictable, and energising chapter in my professional life. We often felt as though we were making it up as we went along, but at the heart of our work was a shared determination to make schools better for kids.

My deep gratitude also extends to my PhD supervisors and my fellow researchers on the ILETC project at the University of Melbourne. Together, we embarked on a bold, collaborative inquiry into innovative learning environments, for deeper learning. Thanks to my supervisors, Associate Professor Wes Imms and Associate Professor Ben Cleveland, and all the dedicated researchers and doctoral colleagues who enriched that journey.

Thank you, Alicia and Andrew from Amba Press; your wise editorial guidance and belief in this project has sustained me, helping to transform these ideas into a resource that can truly serve our important mission. Thank you, Tess McCabe, for your creative cover design.

To my colleagues at The Learning Future, Louka Parry and Amie Fabry, thank you for your ongoing collaboration as we work with schools to imagine and create future-focused learning and professional cultures.

Finally, to those closest to me: Joe and Marissa; Sam, Anneke, Soren, and Rory. Your love and encouragement sustain me in all things. And to Bill – your enduring patience, your constant encouragement, and your unwavering belief in me, even in moments when I doubted myself, made this possible. I could not have reached this point without you. Here's to all the adventures still to come.

Preface

What if school was a place where every learner could thrive, flourish, and explore their passions, a place where imagination, creativity, and divergent thinking were celebrated? For generations, we have perfected a pathway for the conventional academic student and then kept replicating it, hoping that every learner might eventually 'catch on'. But many of the world's most creative and successful minds struggled within this system.

Misfit genius who changed the world: Albert Einstein struggled in school. He found the rigid structure stifling and resented rote learning. Teachers considered him slow and uncooperative, and he was often labelled as a poor student.

Visionary astronomer who defied expectations: British space scientist and broadcaster Maggie Aderin-Pocock struggled with dyslexia and was often dismissed by teachers who doubted her abilities. She was repeatedly told she had no academic future, yet her passion for science and space propelled her forward. She went on to earn a PhD in mechanical engineering and has become a leading astronomer, celebrated for her work on satellites and her ability to inspire the next generation of scientists.

Food campaigner who rewrote the recipe: Jamie Oliver struggled at school because of dyslexia. Dismissed as a failure, he found his path in food. Now a global chef, activist, and *England's bestselling non-fiction author of all time*, Oliver's story underscores the value of practical skills and finding purpose beyond the classroom.

Entrepreneurial visionary who revolutionised travel: Richard Branson, the founder of the Virgin Group, struggled in school. He felt misunderstood and unsupported, eventually dropping out at 16. Branson has credited his entrepreneurial success to qualities like creativity, adaptability, and problem-solving, skills that schools failed to nurture in him.

Trailblazing poet, author, and civil rights icon: The celebrated poet and author Maya Angelou had a difficult time in school, partly due to trauma and a feeling of disconnection. She described herself as a quiet observer, often disengaged from formal education. Through self-guided exploration, books, and mentors outside school, she found her voice and creativity, highlighting the need for learning environments where every child feels seen and valued.

Inventor who was labelled difficult: Thomas Edison, genius inventor of the light bulb and phonograph, was labelled 'difficult' and inattentive in school. Teachers dismissed him as 'addled' (mentally slow), and his mother chose to home-school him. Edison's independent learning and curiosity allowed him to develop the creative mindset that led to over 1,000 inventions.

Best-selling author who found herself outside the classroom: J. K. Rowling, the creator of *Harry Potter*, didn't feel inspired or encouraged during her school years. Though academically capable, she often described her school experience as uninspiring. Rowling's creative gifts blossomed through imagination and determination.

Like them, I struggled with school. I didn't always play by the rules and perhaps you didn't either.

For too long, success in education has been confined to a narrow lens, measured by test scores and exam results. But in a world defined by complexity and rapid change, isn't it time for a new perspective?

If test scores and exam results were no longer the measure of success at school, what might be? Deeper learning – a school culture that values engagement, fostering agency, creativity, and problem-solving skills, essential attributes for an uncertain and rapidly changing world. This field guide explores how we might transform a student's experience of education into a living eco-system, responsive to the needs of every student and every community.

What if...

- *Every school* was a place where *every young person* might find success and belonging, and even catch a glimpse of purpose?
- *Creative minds* could experience an education system built not to confine them but to unleash their potential?
- *Our society* found ways to celebrate and acknowledge success beyond the exam metrics?

This is my professional quest, my *why*:

- To challenge the status quo

- To explore practical pathways for transformation
- To help educators and leaders re-imagine schools
- To create places where all young people, no matter their strengths, passions, or struggles, can belong, grow, and flourish.

Because right now, in classrooms around the world, there are Jamies, Maggies, Mayas, and countless others whose brilliance and creativity need space to thrive. The future depends on the schools we craft for them today.

My challenge to you

If you are satisfied with the traditional, linear model of schooling – where teaching is focused on content and where curriculum delivery is like rolling a ball down a bowling alley, knocking down some pins while others remain untouched – then this resource may not be for you. But if you are discontent with the status quo, keep reading.

This book draws on my PhD research, along with decades working in schools and with schools on change and transformation. As I wrote my thesis, I was tackling the mountain of philosophical and theoretical literature and found my place in complexity theory.

Challenging our assumptions lies at the heart of navigating complexity in our unpredictable world because it allows us to question entrenched beliefs and uncover new perspectives that align with evolving realities. By critically examining what we take for granted, we create space for innovative solutions and adaptive strategies that can address the dynamic and interconnected nature of complex systems. This is my challenge to you. Before we begin, I invite you to pause and reflect on the structures of school we often take for granted:

- The day, the week, the year
- The timetable
- The classroom
- The work of the teacher
- How students learn and experience school
- The role of the principal/leadership
- The physical place.

As you reflect on these aspects of school consider this:

> *What if everything you thought you knew about these was open to disruption?*

This provocation is grounded in the context of my research, which explored the shift from solo to co-teaching as a necessary response to navigating the complexity of contemporary education. In a world where collaboration, adaptability, and responsiveness are increasingly vital, my thesis argued that co-teaching should no longer be a fringe innovation but the default mode of practice. While my research focused specifically on the practice of co-teaching, the broader imperative to disrupt conventional structures is relevant across all aspects of school life. Whether rethinking the teacher's role, the design of the school day, or the architecture of learning itself, embracing complexity invites us to reimagine what school can be.

This is my invitation: to embrace a transformational mindset, to challenge the conventions we've inherited, and to reimagine school as a dynamic environment that prepares students not just for today, but for the rapidly evolving world of tomorrow. Together, let's grasp curiosity, question the status quo, and explore bold new possibilities for the schools of this and future generations.

Reflect and reimagine

1. **Think back to your own school experience.** Were there times when your creativity or strengths felt overlooked? How does that shape how you think about learning today?
2. **How does your school define success?** If exam results were no longer the benchmark, what alternative measures might reflect student growth and achievement?
3. **What role do educators play in shaping thriving learning ecosystems?** How might leadership and teaching practice evolve to support every learner to flourish?
4. **What assumptions about school structures need to be challenged?** Which aspects, like timetables, classrooms, or roles, feel most in need of rethinking?
5. **Imagine a school where every student feels successful and seen.** What core principles or practices would you prioritise – and what's one step you could take today to move toward that vision?

A field guide for transforming schools

Schools today operate in an era of growing complexity and rapid change. Traditional models, shaped by efficiency, compliance, and a narrow definition of success, are increasingly misaligned with the needs of today's learners and the demands of tomorrow's world. As educational leaders, we are not merely managing change; we are actively shaping environments that cultivate adaptability, creativity, and resilience.

This field guide supports your journey with both a conceptual framework and a practical playbook. It is a structured yet flexible resource to help you navigate the complexity of transformation that is unique to your context. This is not a prescriptive model; it acknowledges that transformation is nonlinear, contextual, and deeply relational. Each school begins its journey from a different starting point, shaped by its own culture, people, and wider community.

A field guide, not a blueprint

This resource serves as a strategic compass. It helps you survey your current landscape, identify where you are now, and navigate a future aligned with your vision. Like any great adventure, the route is yours to navigate, the terrain to be mapped.

The process is not about implementing someone else's solution. It is about constructing your own pathway to a school culture that is uniquely yours, through authentic collaboration and empowered leadership. It is a framework for strategic wayfinding, helping you to respond with intention, not reaction.

How it works

The field guide is divided into two parts:

Part 1: Foundations for Change

This lays the intellectual and philosophical groundwork. Drawing on my PhD research and extensive experience working alongside school leaders, teachers, and communities, I explore the conceptual shifts required to move beyond the status quo. This section introduces the core elements that influence holistic school design and transformation:

- **Chapter 1: From Classrooms to Learning Ecosystems.** What if we reimagined schools, not as isolated classrooms but as thriving ecosystems? This chapter invites you to see learning as an interconnected experience, shaped by the relationships between people, the pedagogical approaches we embrace, and the spaces we inhabit. By aligning these three elements – people, pedagogy, and place – we can begin to create environments that foster agency, creativity, and deep engagement for both students and teachers.

- **Chapter 2: Leadership as a Catalyst.** Transformation doesn't happen by chance, or by just tinkering at the edges of 'business as usual', it starts with bold leadership. This chapter explores how leaders are catalysts for meaningful change by aligning vision, shaping culture, and creating the conditions to support new ways of working. Grounded in real examples, this chapter challenges traditional top-down models and invites visionary, distributed leadership that empowers people and builds lasting momentum.

- **Chapter 3: *Samepageness*: Building Alignment and Trust.** Co-teaching isn't just about sharing space; it's about shared purpose. This chapter introduces the concept of samepageness, the intentional alignment of vision, values, and practice. Through compelling metaphors and practical tools, we explore how trust, clarity, and backstage collaboration transform co-teaching into a dynamic, energising force for student success and professional growth.

- **Chapter 4: Agentic Learning Design.** What if learning wasn't something we delivered, but something we designed *with* and *for* students? This chapter repositions teachers as designers of learning, using empathy, iteration, and collaboration to create experiences that foster student ownership and engagement. Drawing on design thinking and real-world examples, it outlines how shifting from rigid lesson plans to adaptive learning design can transform classroom culture and empower learners.

- **Chapter 5: The Power of Place: Rethinking Learning Spaces.** Space shapes behaviour and activity. Our physical environments are not viewed as static containers, but as dynamic partners in education. This chapter introduces spatial literacy and offers strategies for designing flexible, inclusive, and purposeful spaces that reflect and reinforce your school's vision. By aligning space with pedagogy and culture, we can unlock the full potential of learning environments.

Part 1 invites you to challenge your assumptions about teaching, leadership, learning, even the very shape of school, to see your school as a dynamic ecosystem. Each chapter concludes with:

- Reflect and reimagine – questions to discuss
- Practical action – links to tools and ideas from the Playbook.

Part 2: The Playbook

The next part shifts from ideas toward implementation. It is your toolkit for transformation, offering practical resources, collaborative activities, and ready-to-use tools. These tools draw from a range of sources across my professional life: some were developed through my own creativity and practice, some I've learnt from colleagues, while others are acknowledged from their authors. Each tool values the principles of distributed cognition (better together) and collaborative practice (equal voices), supporting shared understanding and shared action.

These tools help you and your team to:

- Make thinking visible and shared
- Navigate complexity using established frameworks from well-known experts
- Foster alignment and co-ownership through design sprints, empathy mapping, and strategic planning
- Create structures that sustain long-term, meaningful change.

You are invited to dip in, to begin with your strategic priority. Use this field guide to support reflection, facilitate professional learning, or scaffold a transformation project. Whether you're stepping into change for the first time or refining a long-term strategy, this field guide is your companion in the mess of change, offering clarity and momentum.

A final word before we begin

Transformation doesn't begin with technology, spatial design, or programs; it begins with leadership, a courageous commitment to question what we take for granted and to reimagine what is possible. 'Transforming schools' are not created by accident, nor is there an end point. They are intentionally designed through vision, trust, and a culture of shared purpose within an ongoing cycle of problem-surfacing and solution-finding.

In complex systems like schools, there is no simple formula or five-step plan that guarantees future success. Schools are living ecosystems which are constantly evolving and shaped by the interplay of people, practice, and place. Transformation begins by identifying a problem worth solving. Problems are not roadblocks; they're opportunities and invitations. They are the gateways to doing things better, doing them differently, and imagining new possibilities. Whether the challenge is cultural, structural, or pedagogical, it holds the potential to catalyse meaningful change.

Progress, in a complex system like a school, is contextualised. For some schools, the path forward might be a bold leap; for others, a single step. What matters is movement. With the strategies presented here, I encourage leaders and teams to embrace problems, make a decision, take action, and learn from the results. Momentum is built through movement, not perfection. Every thoughtful step, however small, is progress.

Here is an invitation to explore, to disrupt, and to create, transforming schools.

Part 1

Foundations for Change

Introduction

My PhD journey was more than an academic pursuit; it became a deeply personal exploration of my career in education. I've long sought to understand and re-imagine education, asking the fundamental yet simple question: *How do we make schools better for kids?*

I still remember the classrooms from my school days. They were rigid, confining, and uninspiring. We were passive recipients, in classrooms bound by compliance, with success measured by our grades. As a teacher, I dared to dream of a different kind of school experience for kids like me.

Why this book

The title intentionally includes the word *transforming*. This signals an ongoing process that recognises that human-centred organisations like schools are never a finished product. They aren't neatly tied up with a bow and presented as complete. Transformation is never a final destination, but a continual act of responsiveness: to learners, to context, and to purpose. This field guide offers provocations, frameworks, and practical strategies to support school communities as they navigate change that is unique to their own context, makes progress at their own pace, and emerges in its own way. The work of transforming is never truly done, and that's what makes it both challenging and full of possibility.

Beyond the status quo

For generations, schools have been structured as hierarchical systems designed to efficiently transmit bounded knowledge as a pathway to employment. However, in today's world, where individuals navigate multiple careers, a content-heavy, exam-driven, and competitive culture is no longer fit for purpose. Instead, we must embrace distributed cognition, essential for addressing complex challenges.

The pursuit of education as individualistic and competitive represents an era past. As Annie Murphy Paul writes in *The Extended Mind: The Power of Thinking Outside the Brain* (2021), 'Individual cognition is simply not sufficient to meet the challenges of the world in which information is so abundant, expertise is so specialized, and issues so complex' (p. 215). An education system that maintains individual cognition as its focus no longer serves our students' future.

It reinforces the 'paradigm of one', as Wright (2017) describes it, a model where one teacher, one class, one classroom, and one subject at a time is replicated for the learner experience and the professional culture. When the future is characterised by learning that is human-centred, connected, and collaborative, this past paradigm is no longer fit for purpose.

The global landscape underscores the urgency of this transformation. In a world characterised by rapid technological advancements, environmental crises, and shifting economic realities, predictable, one-size-fits-all approaches are ill-suited to meet the challenges of our time.

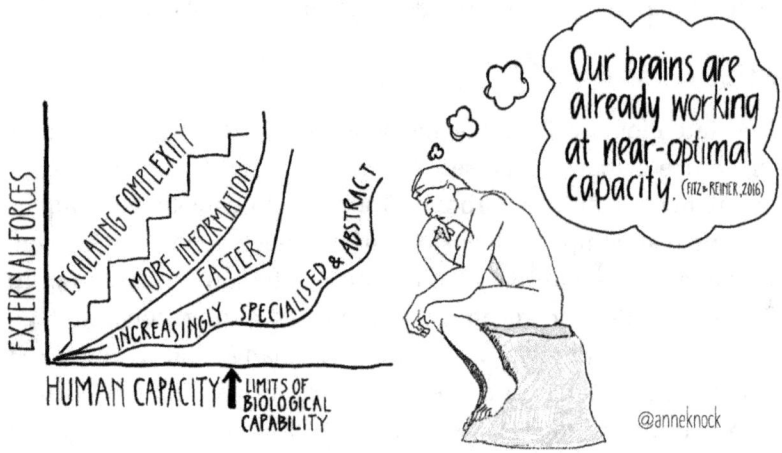

How did I get here? Two pivotal moments and an 'aha'

Every journey of transformation has defining moments, times when a shift in perspective occurs. These challenge long-held assumptions and pave the way for new possibilities. In my journey, two key experiences shaped my understanding of why educational change is necessary. These pivotal moments provided insight into the gap between vision and practice, as well as the enduring structures that hold traditional schooling in place.

Pivotal moment #1

As a self-confessed news and popular culture enthusiast, my attention was captured by a *Time* magazine cover in 2006: *How to Build a Student for the 21st Century*. Inside, the article 'How to bring our schools out of the 20th century' repurposed the fairy tale of Rip Van Winkle, who fell asleep in 1906 and woke up a century later. Everything was foreign – hospitals, airports, shopping malls – until Rip walked into a school. Recognising the familiar setup, he exclaimed: 'This is a school! We used to have these back in 1906. Only now the blackboards are green.' Then this comment struck me:

> Kids spend much of the day as their great-grandparents once did: sitting in rows, listening to teachers lecture, scribbling notes by hand, reading from textbooks that are out of date by the time they are printed. A yawning chasm (with an emphasis on yawning) separates the world inside the schoolhouse from the world outside.

It was a true penny-drop moment. I realised that the first decade of the 21st century, with evolving technology, was a pivotal time in history. The internet was in its infancy, and things were beginning to shift. Now, two decades later, a quarter of the way into the 21st century, we're still having the same conversations; only now, the focus has shifted from the internet to AI.

Pivotal moment #2

The next pivotal moment in my professional journey occurred during two visits to a Scandinavian school. The first visit, shortly after its completion, showcased an intentional, future-focused design. It had large multi-cohort areas, flexible breakout rooms, and varied furniture, all crafted to foster student agency, collaborative teaching, and diverse learning opportunities. One standout space, a light-filled breakout area with a café-like atmosphere, exemplified how environments can accommodate a variety of learning modalities and social connection. This visit was prior to commencement.

Eighteen months later, I returned to find a starkly different reality. The school had been operating for about one year and the initial design-vision had been dismantled. Collaborative shared spaces had became closed, corralled by bookcases and cupboards. Teachers appeared unaware of the design intention and its pedagogical potential. This misalignment between leadership vision, teacher practice, and the physical environment highlighted a critical gap: *the need to equip educators to align their culture and practices with the opportunities afforded by innovative spaces.* The spaces we inhabit reflect our beliefs about learning and professional practice.

As illustrated in the photos below, the vibrant light-filled learning space had been transformed into a dark, enclosed area, visually capturing the disconnect between design intent and everyday practice.

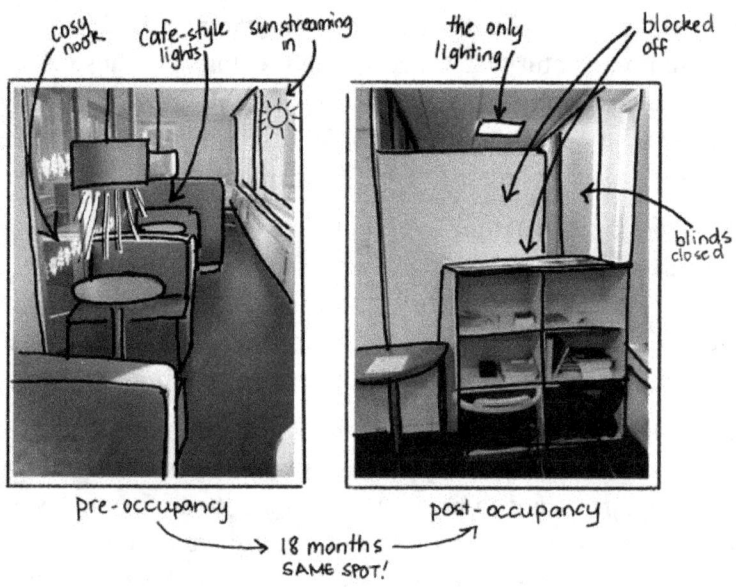

This experience became a catalyst for my work with schools, revealing the risks of relying on contemporary architectural design without ensuring alignment with supporting educational practices and a complementary professional culture. It reinforced the importance of shared vision, reimagining the student experience, and equipping teachers to connect professional practice and physical design. This foundation, central to my PhD research, underscores the interplay of adaptable design, cultural alignment, and transformative leadership as pillars for sustainable change.

The 'aha' moment: breaking free from the *paradigm of one*

On a post-PhD visit to a school in Copenhagen, I met Claus, a headteacher whose passion for innovation and collaboration was unmistakable. As he described the co-teaching culture that defines his school, he said something that struck a deep chord:

> 'Teaching is too complex to do it alone.'

After years of researching what makes innovative learning environments successful and sustainable, his words resonated profoundly. They captured what I had come to see as a fundamental truth: the traditional solo-teaching model, the *paradigm of one*, must be disrupted for schools to truly transform.

A decade earlier, this realisation piqued my curiosity, which ultimately led to PhD research into what factors influence the positive long-term impact of workplace change for teachers in innovative learning environments. My thesis, titled *The Beauty of a Complex Future: Redefining Teacher Success and Sustainability in Innovative Learning Environments*, underscored the need for schools to embrace cultural shifts that redefine what it means to teach and work together. I concluded that redefining teachers' professional culture from predominantly solo to co-teaching as the norm is one of the most significant workplace changes educators will face in the future. That is, if there is a will to change.

While the autonomy of the solo-teacher model may offer control, I found that it limits collaboration, innovation, and adaptability – the very qualities that are essential for the future. Through my research into successful and sustainable practices in innovative learning environments, it became clear that transitioning from the *paradigm of one* to a collaborative, team-based approach is far more than a logistical adjustment. It is a profound cultural transformation.

Co-teaching as cultural transformation

Shifting from solo to co-teaching challenges long-standing assumptions about the student experience of school and what it means to be a teacher. It requires educators to work together in proximity in shared spaces. Here they align their goals and adapt to each other and engage in new ways of designing and presenting learning. It represents a significant departure from the traditional role of the teacher, which has long prioritised individual responsibility over collective accountability. It demands not only new skills but a fundamental shift in the professional culture.

In my research, I found that this transition presents both opportunities and challenges. Teachers who embraced co-teaching described it as professionally energising, explaining how working alongside colleagues enhanced their practice, deepened their professional satisfaction, and broadened what they could offer to students.

Yet enthusiasm alone is not enough to sustain this shift. It depends on a professional culture that prioritises trust, shared processes, and collaboration as much as the individual expertise each person brings. Without these foundations, co-teaching can falter, leaving teachers feeling overwhelmed or disconnected. Differences in teaching philosophies, communication styles, and decision-making approaches can create tension if not intentionally addressed.

Successful co-teaching cultures embrace open dialogue, shared professional learning, and clearly defined roles that evolve over time. By fostering a culture of shared responsibility and continuous collaboration, schools can ensure that co-teaching becomes a sustainable and impactful practice.

Ultimately, the move from traditional solo-teaching models to becoming team-based is not merely a structural change, but a cultural transformation. Schools that embrace this shift position themselves to better support both teachers and students in an evolving educational landscape.

With this understanding of co-teaching as a cultural and professional shift, we now turn our attention to the broader foundation of transformative learning environments. In the next chapter, we explore how people, pedagogy, and place intersect to create learning ecosystems that are innovative, sustainable, and responsive to the future.

Reflect and reimagine

1. **Have you ever felt limited by the *paradigm of one*?** Reflect on how traditional models of teaching or learning have impacted your experience or professional growth.
2. **What are the biggest barriers to co-teaching in your school?** Consider the cultural, structural, or leadership obstacles that hinder collaborative approaches.
3. **What might foster a culture of collaboration?** Identify key actions, practices, or spatial strategies that would help embed collaboration.
4. **What assumptions about teaching need to be challenged?** Which beliefs about teachers' roles or classroom structures may be limiting transformation?
5. **Design your transforming school.** If collaboration were central, what values, spaces, and practices would you prioritise?

Chapter 1
From Classrooms to Learning Ecosystems

Now we will explore the foundation of transformative learning environments, highlighting how people, pedagogy, and place interconnect to create innovative and sustainable learning environments.

Building on the foundational concepts of deeper learning through the lens of complexity, we examine how empowered individuals, spatial design, and pedagogy work in harmony to foster agency, collaboration, and creativity. By exploring this interplay, we uncover actionable strategies for reimagining schools as adaptive, future-focused environments that prepare students and teachers for an unpredictable world.

The core elements of transformative learning environments

People, pedagogy, and place are intertwined; they are key to meaningful and adaptive teaching and learning. The alignment of these dimensions forms the foundation of effective learning environments, where collaboration, agency, and creativity take centre stage in student and teacher experience.

But first, let's make sure we are on the same page, with a shared understanding of what we mean by 'learning environment'. Rather than treating it only as a modern rebrand of the *classroom*, the term *learning environment* is used here to describe an ecosystem, a dynamic space where deeper learning occurs, which takes into consideration:

- The community: educators, leaders, students, and families
- The pedagogical context: professional culture, teaching, and learning activities
- The physical place: design, affordances, and how these enable deeper learning.

Learning environments evolve through the intentional alignment of people, place, and pedagogy, enabling sustainable, adaptive learning.

People: the human heart of transformation

At the core of every learning environment are the students, teachers, leaders, and broader community who together bring it to life. Relationships, roles, responsibilities, and social connections define the human ecosystem of schools. Educators play a vital role in fostering a culture that enables learning and social connection. Ultimately, culture relates to people, and people are the essence of a school's identity, purpose, and potential for transformation. Buildings, curriculum, and pedagogy are the vehicles that serve the people.

Student agency for engagement

Through an agentic learning lens, students are active participants rather than passive recipients of knowledge. Student agency involves giving learners voice and choice around how, what, and why they learn. Growing agentic learners requires a shared culture, envisioned by leaders, and co-created by educators. This approach involves:

- **Empowering through agency:** Learners thrive when they feel ownership and a connection to learning, where they are empowered as decision-makers.
- **Designing for diversity:** Rather than a one-size experience, design deepens educators' understanding of student needs and motivations, ensuring inclusive learning experiences.
- **Facilitating transfer:** A holistic education emphasises deeper learning. It moves beyond memorisation to pass the test, and toward critical thinking, problem-solving, and collaboration as life-long skills that can be transferred across perspectives.

'Agentic learning' is a key term in this book. At its core, it recognises learners as unique individuals who feel valued and capable, and are encouraged to initiate learning, becoming explorers.

This way of understanding the learner lies at the heart of transforming the professional culture. The student experience is enhanced by co-teaching, presenting an authentic, collaborative approach that models the skills we seek to grow in students.

In their book *The Disengaged Teen: Helping Kids Learn Better, Feel Better, and Live Better* (2025), Jenny Anderson and Rebecca Winthrop focus on students' engagement and agency. Engagement is not just about what students get done but also how they feel about themselves as learners; it's influenced by their sense of belonging and connection. Agency, they explain, requires self-knowledge: 'How do I learn best? What distracts me? What motivates me? What do I care about?' (p. 16). Student agency is demonstrated in their capacity and willingness to initiate, creating a growing awareness of their own learning interests and needs.

From solo to co-teaching

My research focused on the attributes of successful and sustainable co-teaching. My own teaching practice was mostly in settings that represented the formal solo model of teaching. However, my most rewarding experiences were the informal collaboration with colleagues as we shared practice, despite the walls that separated us. Working alongside another teacher not only broadened our collective capacity, but also strengthened collegiality and was professionally energising.

Shifting from solo to co-teaching is a cultural transformation; it means adopting new ways of working that prioritise authentic collaboration, shared responsibility, and collective growth. Key shifts in teacher roles include:

1. **From solo to team:** Co-teaching requires intentional alignment of vision, values, and practices, supported by structured collaboration and professional learning.
2. **Prioritising social capital:** Trust and communication are the cornerstones of collaboration. Co-teaching agreements and shared reflection sessions strengthen these bonds.
3. **Embracing design mindset:** Teachers become designers, iterating their professional practice based on student feedback and outcomes.

In both my teaching experience and my research, I found that when teachers were well-supported and embraced co-teaching, it was professionally energising. Many who transition to this model express a renewed sense of collegiality and creativity, stating that they would not want to return to the isolation of solo teaching.

One final word from Anderson and Winthrop as they reflect on the demands placed on teaching in this complex world: 'The job is not humanly possible...

This structure, one teacher, one classroom – it's a model that has to change' (p. 20).

This shift also demands a reconsideration of the physical spaces where teaching occurs. Just as pedagogy evolves, so too must the physical environments that support it.

Place: the transformative power of space

The place where learning occurs actively shapes interactions, behaviours, and engagement. Spatial design plays a critical role in fostering connections, collaboration, and creativity.

Finding affordances

Affordances refer to the possibilities for action that a space provides. For example, expected affordances of a window include allowing light in and offering a view. An unexpected affordance might be its use as a writable surface. In learning spaces:

- Whiteboard walls afford spontaneous brainstorming and collaboration.
- Lightweight furniture affords adaptability and spontaneous grouping.
- Quiet alcoves afford individual and uninterrupted focus.

Growing spatial literacy is essential – a muscle to be exercised and developed. It leads to a deeper understanding of how physical environments align with pedagogical goals to optimise student engagement. Yet, in many cases, pre-service education and ongoing professional development on spatial affordances is lacking, leading to unrealised potential.

Flexibility and inclusivity

Learning spaces need to accommodate diverse pedagogical approaches and student needs. Designing for inclusivity and adaptability means incorporating principles such as:

- Movable furniture and modular layouts for adaptability
- Writable surfaces for collaborative engagement
- Sensory-friendly zones for neurodiverse learners
- Transparent elements, such as glass walls, to foster connection and visibility.

Inclusivity extends beyond meeting the accessibility compliance requirements. Thoughtful design accommodates diverse learning needs, ensuring every individual feels valued and empowered. Such spaces support deeper learning and collaboration. Integrating nature into design enhances wellbeing, engagement, and cognitive performance.

Biophilic design and wellbeing

Research increasingly supports incorporating biophilic design, an approach that connects people with nature by integrating natural elements such as light, greenery, and organic materials. In *Good Nature: The New Science of How Nature Improves Our Health*, Kathy Willis (2024) explains that in hospitals 'just the *sight* of plants can have direct positive impacts on the patients' health' (p. 4).

In learning environments, these features positively influence cognitive, emotional, and social outcomes. Key principles include:

- **Natural light:** Improves mood, wellbeing, and cognitive performance.
- **Greenery and living elements:** Gardens, living walls, and outdoor views enhance psychological and physiological wellbeing.
- **Nature-inspired materials:** Wood, stone, and biomimicry in design evoke essential connections to nature.
- **Outdoor learning spaces:** Access to fresh air, vegetation, and natural sounds can reduce stress and improve focus.

Outdoor classrooms, transition zones with nature integration, and simple additions like plants or nature-inspired artwork can make a meaningful impact. Willis also highlights studies related to the school environment and impact on learning, suggesting 'that views of nature improve our cognitive functioning because of the restorative effect that they have on our directed attention' (p. 23). The strategic use of natural elements fosters a sense of calm and belonging, supporting both student and teacher wellbeing.

Design on purpose

For many of us, when we were students, our classroom 'design' was purely functional, reflecting the *paradigm of one*. However, the evolving understanding of how space impacts learning necessitates a more intentional approach. Thoughtful design creates zones for different learning purposes, moving away from the restrictive and replicated egg-crate model of the traditional classroom.

Thoughtful design supports a range of pedagogical practices by creating distinct zones that can allow for learning that is teacher-directed, teacher-supported, and student-initiated. This flexibility ensures that learning environments cater to diverse needs, allowing students to move fluidly between modes. Intentional zoning fosters engagement, autonomy, and a greater sense of ownership over learning experiences, ensuring that space proactively supports pedagogical goals rather than constrains them.

Pedagogy: designing for deeper learning

Pedagogy, the art, science, and practice of teaching, serves as the foundation for engaging students, fostering critical thinking, and adapting to diverse needs. Deeper learning is at the heart of people, pedagogy, and place, creating adaptive learning environments and moving beyond the teach-test-repeat cycle.

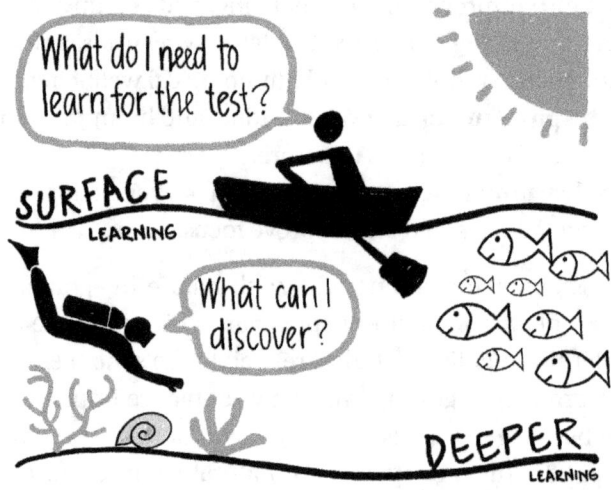

Deeper learning prioritises understanding and cognitive engagement. This is in contrast to surface learning, which on its own is driven by extrinsic motivation and short-term goals such as passing tests. Researchers including Marton and Säljö (1976) and Biggs (1988) explored a qualitative approach to measuring learning that went beyond test scores. These and other researchers found that deeper learning is characterised by intrinsic motivation, curiosity, and meaning-making. Further contributions from Hattie and Donoghue (2016) introduced the idea of a learning continuum, valuing surface knowledge acquisition as a critical foundation to deeper learning, culminating in transfer, the ability to apply knowledge to new contexts. Valuing knowledge remains important, not as an end in itself, but as a means to developing learner capacity.

Thoughtful spatial design offers affordances that encourage a shift from predominantly teacher-led practices to teacher-supported and student-initiated pedagogies. They are not merely containers for human activity but are active participants in creating a deeper learning culture. Aligning physical design with pedagogical intent can disrupt potentially constraining traditional models and grow a culture of deeper learning, ultimately equipping students with the dispositions and competencies needed to navigate and contribute meaningfully in a complex and changing world.

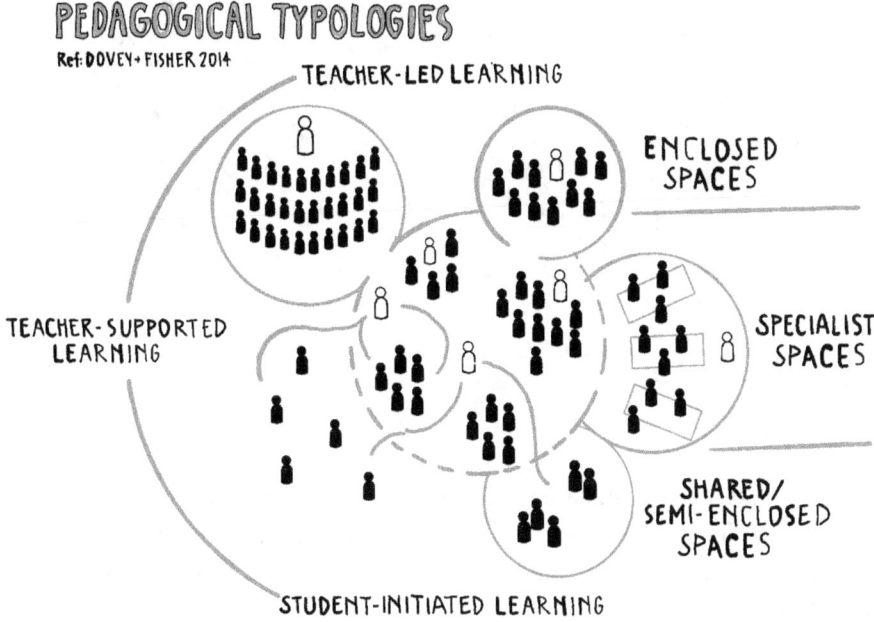

To foster deeper learning, the pedagogical repertoire expands beyond *teacher-led learning* as the predominant practice, aligning strategies with spatial affordances, student needs, and curriculum requirements. The potential for the space is broadened to incorporate *teacher-supported learning* and *student-initiated learning*. Creating an effective environment for deeper learning means that we think deeply about using the affordances and spaces available to greater effect. This requires thinking like a designer.

Becoming designers

Adopting a design mindset is a game-changer in the interplay of people, place, and pedagogy for deeper learning. Designers think holistically about a problem. In *How Designers Think: The Design Process Demystified*, Lawson (2006) responds to the problem of a broken doorknob. We could just fix the doorknob, or we could begin to think about the opportunities: *Do we actually need a door?* and *Do we even need the walls?* Design helps us develop a wider definition of the problem.

We are often more cognisant of design in the physical and material sense. Yet, crafting learning experiences that are personal for students is also the subject of design, enabling a more integrated response, rather than a siloed or immediate fix (*the doorknob is broken*).

In an objectively evidence-driven world like education, how might we apply a seemingly subjective approach like design to student learning, one that incorporates the lived experience of educators? Abductive reasoning becomes a both/and approach that allows us to make informed decisions by drawing on both empirical data (inductive/evidence-informed) and professional judgment (deductive/lived experience-informed), because both matter.

Abductive reasoning is closely aligned with the processes of design. Implementing design-led strategies can draw on relevant evidence, observation, student feedback, and evolving classroom dynamics. A sample design cycle – notice, define, ideate, and prototype – illustrates the iterative, reflective approach that is central to educators-as-designers.

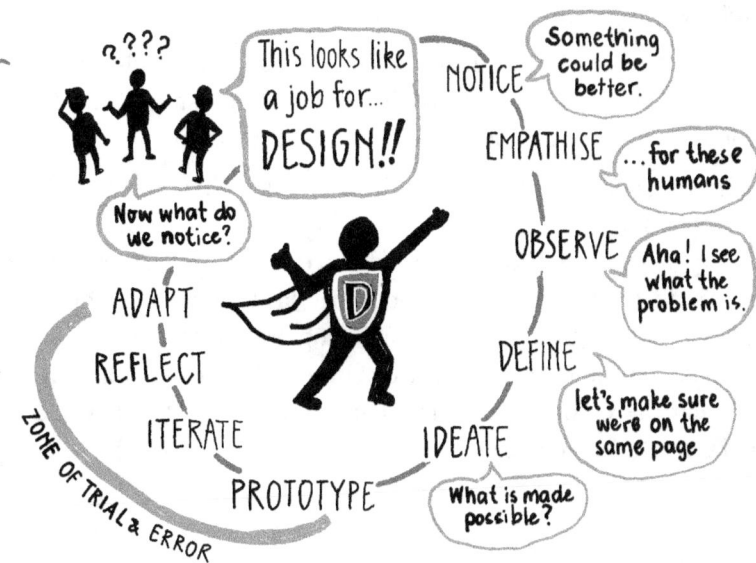

The design deep-dive requires taking time to gain a greater understanding of the context of the learner. As I found from my research, the co-teachers in the innovative learning environment valued the 'zone of trial and error' as they grappled with the complexity of their professional context.

By viewing ourselves as designers, we can move beyond traditional, linear constructs, instead iterating and refining practices to meet dynamic learning needs. This mindset encourages:

- Designing learning experiences that spark curiosity and sustain student interest
- Leveraging spatial affordances to align learning with the broader pedagogical goals
- Applying design thinking principles such as empathy, ideation, and iteration.

Together, these elements empower educators to craft dynamic and responsive learning environments, ensuring that both pedagogical strategies and spatial design work in harmony to enhance student engagement and success.

The interplay of people, place, and pedagogy

The potential to transform schools into cohesive ecosystems is critical, as we shift from siloed thinking. When aligned, students can be empowered, teachers can thrive in professional collegiality, and spaces amplify learning possibilities.

To achieve this alignment, leaders strategically guide culture, equip educators, and align efforts across the school ecosystem. This foundation supports deeper learning, adaptability, and innovation.

The following chapters will explore these elements in greater depth, unpacking how they shape transformative learning environments. However, the next chapter on leadership is pivotal, as effective leadership serves as the driving force behind this alignment. Without strong, visionary leadership, efforts to create transforming schools risk being fragmented or unsustainable. Effective leaders champion a culture of innovation, foster collaboration, and ensure that the vision for people, place, and pedagogy is realised at every level of the school ecosystem.

Reflect and reimagine

1. **Think back to a time you experienced agency, collaboration, or adaptability:** What made that environment successful or where did you encounter barriers?
2. **How does your school currently think about its 'learning environment'?** What spatial or structural changes could better align with your pedagogical goals?
3. **How does your current culture enable or inhibit collaboration?** What leadership actions or shared practices would strengthen collective ownership?
4. **What assumptions about teaching or spatial design might need disrupting?** Which traditions are holding your practice or setting back?
5. **Imagine your transforming school:** What's one principle, space, or structure you'd prioritise – and one step you could take today?

Practical action

- **Breaking Down Silos** (p. 145): Move beyond isolated practice by creating cross-disciplinary collaboration opportunities, fostering integrated curriculum design, and building stronger, more connected professional cultures.
- **Affordances A–Z** (p. 165): Explore and apply the concept of affordances, the characteristics that spaces invite or enable, to collaboratively design responsive, inclusive learning environments that align with pedagogical purpose and enhance student engagement.
- **Regenerative Ecocycle** (p. 140): Map how time and energy are invested across the school ecosystem – revealing what to sustain, redesign, or let go to foster continuous renewal and purposeful evolution.
- **Impact Map** (p. 110): This reflective tool helps leadership teams evaluate the effects of change initiatives on staff culture and wellbeing – surfacing what's working, what's straining, and where to focus energy for greater impact.

Chapter 2
Leadership as a Catalyst

Transformation begins with effective leadership – articulating vision, shaping culture, resourcing change, and empowering practice.

The posture of leadership: moving beyond hierarchy

The way leaders position themselves in relation to their teams profoundly influences the culture of a school. Traditional leadership models often rely on hierarchical structures, where decisions flow from the top, and teachers are expected to implement policies with little voice in the decision-making. While this approach seemingly provides clarity and order, it can also limit innovation, stifle professional growth, and discourage teachers from taking ownership of their practice.

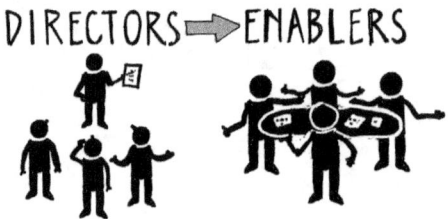

Transformational leaders, by contrast, shift from directing change to enabling professional agency. Effective leaders cultivate an environment of trust, professional autonomy, and collective responsibility, where people take meaningful risks and experiment with new ways of working. This shift requires leaders to distribute responsibility by providing opportunities for growth. These understood parameters provide a framework that supports coherence while preserving creativity.

In my research, Elizabeth, one of the principals, exemplified this approach. She was leading a school transitioning to a new facility with a co-teaching learning environment. Her leadership practices were characterised by flexibility and the encouragement of teacher agency and autonomy.

Leadership in action

Elizabeth's leadership approach was grounded in trust, adaptability, and a clear vision of transformation. Tasked with supporting teachers and students to move into a newly designed co-teaching space, she realised that the traditional hierarchical model of leadership was unsuited. Instead, Elizabeth embraced a bottom-up approach, encouraging the teachers to play an active role in shaping their pedagogy and practice. From this, five core leadership principles emerged as I analysed the data.

1. Safe to try

Elizabeth deliberately created a culture where risk-taking was encouraged. She recognised that this process would challenge teachers to step out of their comfort zones. To alleviate fear and promote experimentation, she established a simple yet powerful norm: *Trial, fail, and be open about failures.*

This reframed setbacks as learning opportunities rather than as indicators of incompetence. Teachers were given permission to innovate without fear, which in turn fostered greater ownership. When the teachers felt safe to take risks, they were more likely to test new strategies, reflect openly, and collectively refine their approaches.

2. In this together

Rather than imposing a predetermined model for the new learning environment, Elizabeth included the teachers in the design process from the outset:

- Encouraging input from them into the physical layout of the new spaces, ensuring that the design complemented their pedagogical needs, rather than dictating her own ideas to them
- Setting up a prototyping space in the old building, so teachers could begin to apply and iterate their ideas
- Prioritising team-based collaborative sessions in the timetable – scheduling weekly sessions for teachers to determine how best to leverage the spaces for student learning.

By embedding teacher agency, Elizabeth fostered a sense of ownership and investment. The teachers were not merely adapting to change; they were actively shaping it.

3. We are all learners

Recognising that autonomy must be supported by capacity-building, Elizabeth invested in professional development as a team. She ensured that teachers:

- Attended workshops together to learn about collaborative and inquiry teaching models
- Visited schools with contemporary designs and professional practice models, providing practical exposure to how others navigated the new learning context
- Had access to peer mentoring structures, where experienced educators supported colleagues in adopting new practices.

These initiatives ensured that teachers felt confident in their evolving roles and that their autonomy was grounded in knowledge and shared understanding.

4. Growing leaders

Elizabeth flattened traditional organisational hierarchies. Instead of making all decisions herself, she restructured the leadership model, appointing teacher-leaders. These were experienced educators who facilitated communication, decision-making, and professional collaboration, circumventing the normal practice. Teacher leaders:

- Served as bridges between staff and leadership, ensuring that feedback from the co-teaching teams informed strategic decisions
- Helped to mediate challenges and supported colleagues in navigating the new environment
- Reinforced the idea that leadership is not about authority, but fostering collective progress of the team.

By embedding leadership within teaching teams, Elizabeth strengthened collaborative decision-making and reinforced the school's commitment to distributed leadership.

5. Leading with agility

While Elizabeth was driven by a bold vision, she also demonstrated agility in responding to immediate needs. One example of this adaptability was her willingness to modify the structure of the classes in the multi-cohort space.

Initially, she had envisioned a fully fluid model, where students would move seamlessly between teachers rather than being assigned to a single home-class teacher. However, teachers expressed their concerns, requesting a base for students, especially at the start of the day and for parent communication.

Instead of enforcing her original plan, Elizabeth:

- Listened to feedback
- Adjusted the structure to accommodate the preference for home-base teachers, providing a balance between flexibility and stability
- Maintained her broader vision while understanding the needs of her team.

This responsiveness reinforced trust. The teachers saw that their voices mattered, making them more willing to engage in future iterations of change.

Moving from control to empowerment

Elizabeth's approach serves as a model for leaders seeking to move beyond hierarchical decision-making. When a leader's default is to operate within rigid, top-down structures, we often feel like passive implementers rather than active contributors. By contrast, leaders who cultivate trust, collaboration, and professional autonomy enable teachers to engage deeply, take ownership, and innovate.

Empowering teachers is not about removing leadership but redefining it. Transforming schools require leaders who see themselves as enablers, not controllers, as architects of culture, not enforcers of compliance. When teachers experience true agency, they in turn create learning environments where students can also develop autonomy, adaptability, and a sense of ownership over their learning.

Thus, the posture of leadership determines the depth of transformation. Schools that embrace relational and responsive leadership, as demonstrated by Elizabeth, are more likely to sustain meaningful change, navigate complexity, and thrive in an unpredictable future.

Challenging taken-for-granted assumptions

Leading transformation begins with challenging tightly-held assumptions about education. Historically, schools have operated within an industrial framework, prioritising standardisation, efficiency, and hierarchical structures. This model, shaped by 19th- and 20th-century industrial practices, was designed for a predictable world, where uniform outputs and lifelong employment were the norm. More than a century later, this approach no longer serves our dynamic and complex reality.

Critical questions emerge about maintaining rigid subject hierarchies, one-size-fits-all pedagogies which reinforce an over-reliance on teacher-led instruction, and the compartmentalisation of learning spaces, reminiscent of the past. These structures, intended for conformity, can limit creativity, adaptability, and student agency required for the future.

As Harari (2018) argues in *21 Lessons for the 21st Century*, much of what students learn today will likely be irrelevant by 2050. This presents a sobering reality for the content-heavy, exam-driven school culture. Despite the rapid changes in the world, many young people still experience education through the lens of the industrial model.

Industrial vs biologic models of leadership

The transforming school moves from an industrial model, characterised by linearity, predictability, and efficiency, to a biologic model that resembles an ecosystem. The industrial model emphasises control and compliance, whereas a biologic model fosters adaptability, self-organisation, and interdependence.

Leaders who adopt a biologic perspective create adaptive spaces where diverse ideas converge, allowing innovation and new solutions to emerge. Schools operating in this mode function like ecosystems, where students, teachers, and community members interact dynamically across different scales. Unlike hierarchical structures, biologic systems thrive on distributed leadership and collaborative decision-making.

This doesn't diminish the essential role of executive leadership. Ultimately, leaders do need to make decisions for the good of the community. However, a culture where voices are heard and perspectives understood builds trust when on-high decisions need to be made. No system is perfect, but a human-centred culture is the optimal starting point. An intentional focus on growing the desired culture requires leaders to strategically create environments where new ways of thinking are welcome.

Not all problems are created equal

In a time of rapid change and unpredictable challenges, school leaders must navigate an increasingly complex landscape. The Cynefin Framework, developed by Dave Snowden (Snowden & Boone, 2007), offers a valuable lens for sense-making across different types of situations.

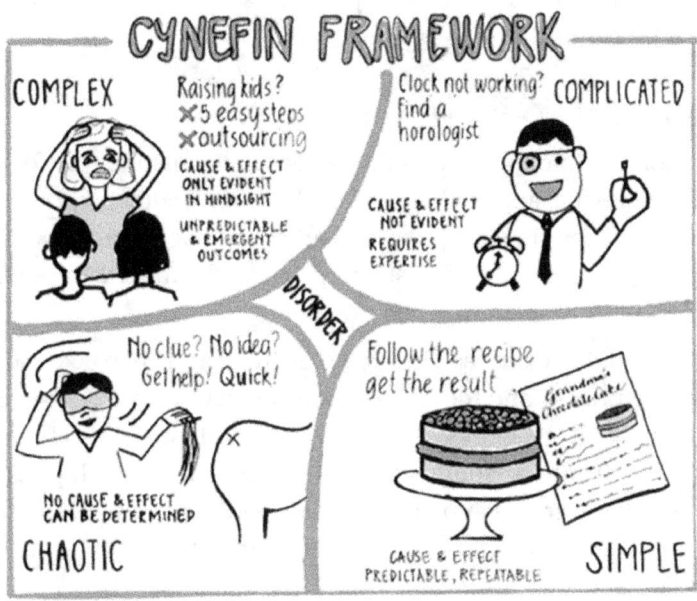

The framework distinguishes between four elements: simple, complicated, complex, and chaotic. In the simple domain, cause-and-effect relationships are clear and repeatable and best-practice models can be applied. Complicated contexts, while requiring expertise and analysis, still yield to logical reasoning and linear problem-solving. However, the terrain shifts dramatically when we enter the complex or chaotic. The Cynefin Framework helps to distinguish between problems that are linear and those that require adaptive, iterative responses.

Many of our problems are mistakenly treated as if they are complicated when they are in fact complex. In the complex domain, outcomes cannot be predicted with certainty, and cause and effect are only understood in retrospect. Here, we must *probe, sense,* and *respond,* allowing patterns to emerge rather than imposing solutions. Snowden emphasises that in these contexts, solutions are not discovered through analysis but through interaction and iteration. Attempts to apply linear, best-practice models to open-ended problems often result in frustration and stagnation. Instead, complexity calls for approaches that are adaptive, participatory, and comfortable with ambiguity.

Recognising the type of problem we face is only the beginning; how we respond reveals our leadership maturity. This is where regenerative leadership offers a path beyond problem-solving, towards cultivating conditions for continual renewal and growth.

Leading regeneratively

Regeneration is a biological system that occurs in nature. The focus is on restoring and revitalising so that systems become healthier, more resilient, and capable of thriving over time. Leading regeneratively means going beyond just maintaining or sustaining what already exists, to actively restoring, renewing, and improving the system.

To lead regeneratively is to lead in a way that gives more than takes, nurturing people, communities, and the environment so they grow stronger, healthier, and more resilient over time. On the other hand, sustainable leadership aims to maintain the existing system. Regenerative leadership presents a deliberate shift toward creating conditions where life can thrive and evolve. Schools are living systems, not machines, with a focus on deep purpose, relationships, and long-term viability.

This approach to leadership prioritises the need to disrupt traditional paradigms and challenge entrenched assumptions. For example, when schools implement multi-cohort learning spaces, where co-teachers work together, new ways of working must be intentionally designed – the old can't be made to fit. Simply placing teachers together in a shared space does not automatically lead to effective co-teaching and collaboration. Proximity alone is insufficient; deliberate time must be allocated to grow capacity and ensure alignment.

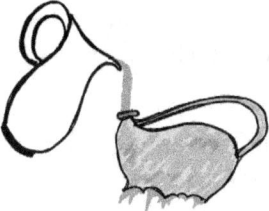

The idea is captured in a biblical analogy – *new wine in old wineskins* – which illustrates how fresh, dynamic ideas can struggle or fail when forced into outdated or rigid structures. Originally, this analogy referred to the way fermenting new wine would burst old, inflexible leather skins. In the same way, regenerative leadership requires new ways of thinking, organising, and leading, with flexible 'containers' that can expand, adapt, and support meaningful transformation.

Leading regeneratively requires more than a shift in mindset; it must be embedded in the daily operations, relationships, and routines of school life. This starts with intentionally shaping the culture and climate. When leaders prioritise trust, collaboration, and shared purpose, they lay the groundwork for the kinds of environments where regenerative principles can take root and thrive. The next step is understanding how culture and climate influence the human experience of school every day.

Culture and climate

A well-articulated vision serves as a unifying force, uniting the school community around a shared purpose. It connects people, pedagogy, and place, ensuring coherence across the life of a school. Vision provides both clarity and direction. It functions as a compass, guiding schools through challenges and enabling them to embrace emerging opportunities with confidence.

School climate is the overall atmosphere of a school, shaped by the quality of relationships, expectations, and the sense of safety and belonging felt by students and staff. It reflects a school's culture in action, revealing how the underlying values, norms, and beliefs are experienced day-to-day by those within the community.

While culture and climate are interconnected, they offer distinct perspectives on a school's environment. Culture, as explained by Schein (2009), 'is a pattern of shared tacit assumptions that was learned by the group as it solved its problems'. It represents the shared and implicit values that drive behaviour and decisions. Climate echoes the lived experiences and perceptions of those within the school.

Educational researcher Neil Gislason (2010) emphasises that 'school design should be viewed as part of a network of elements that together shape the learning environment'. The elements – *learner experience, professional culture, management and systems,* and *places, spaces, and resources* – create a cohesive and intentional way of understanding the learning environment. When these elements are in harmony, they not only shape a strong school culture but also foster a positive school climate, impacting the day-to-day experience of that culture, as lived by the community characterised by a shared purpose.

Future-oriented leaders centre their vision on the people within the school community. They focus on developing a culture that grows deeper learning, student engagement, and professional adaptability, where spaces are shaped to reinforce these principles. The learning environments reflect and enable the school's educational philosophy.

In schools, leaders play a pivotal role as *culture builders*, shaping the shared vision, values, and norms that define a school's identity and guide its practices. Teachers and staff, in turn, serve as *culture bearers*, living out these shared understandings in their daily interactions and work. Strategically cultivating this dynamic relationship ensures that school culture is a reliable constant amid other changing variables, especially for the students. For innovation to take root, leaders align new initiatives with these cultural markers, inclusively leveraging the collective expertise of staff to embed and sustain transformation.

Effective leaders recognise that shaping a strong culture begins with critically examining existing values and how they manifest in daily practice. When values are misaligned or unspoken, leaders can guide the community toward a refreshed set of shared principles, creating coherence and instilling confidence during times of change. This process requires not only establishing common goals but also cultivating an environment of trust and agency. By decentralising control and fostering non-hierarchical collaboration, leaders welcome initiative, allowing innovation to emerge organically within the school.

A strong cultural foundation enables schools to positively navigate complexity, offering both clarity and adaptability. This can be cultivated through *enabling constraints* offering clear guidelines that provide sufficient structure without stifling creativity. These guardrails balance coherence with flexibility, ensuring that both individual and collective efforts remain aligned with the school's vision. Ultimately, a culture rooted in trust, collaboration, and shared purpose positions schools to thrive in complex and evolving educational landscapes, where bottom-up initiative can drive regenerative transformation.

Resourcing the future

Resourcing plays a pivotal role in realising the vision for student learning and an empowered teacher culture. The provision of sufficient resources is a leadership responsibility. Effective resourcing extends beyond financial efficiencies to the deliberate allocation of time for essentials that are inherently interconnected and critical to the vision.

While financial resourcing may vary across schools, *time* remains a universal constant and constraint, making its strategic optimisation crucial. For example, for co-teaching to thrive, a commitment of time for professional collaboration is prioritised in the timetable and makes a difference to team efficacy and working relationships. This includes weekly sessions for iteration and reflection, as well as longer scheduled sessions for strategic design.

Simple yet effective practices can ensure time is used effectively: 15-minute stand-up meetings at the start of each day can align team members, then longer (two-hour) sessions can be scheduled within the timetable for a design deep-dive. It is this intentional allocation of *together time* that acts as an enabling constraint, protecting it from being overtaken by administrative demands and ensuring that strategic use of time directly supports the school's shared vision and co-teachers' effectiveness.

Prioritising collaborative time and providing clarity on how time might be utilised within an already demanding school schedule requires a critical examination of existing practice, asking: *Is everything necessary?* This can begin with assessing how staff time outside of teaching responsibilities might be utilised to greater effect. Reflecting on and auditing routine practice, such as the structure and purpose of weekly staff meetings, can prompt valuable insights:

- Are these meetings aligned with the school priorities?
- Do they harness the collective intelligence in the room, or are they primarily vehicles for information dissemination?

- Are we meeting only because that's what we do, that's what schools have always done?

Challenging long-standing assumptions about these routines can open opportunities to reimagine them in ways that better support the aspiration of the culture.

Strategic resourcing encompasses both time and financial investment and is essential for supporting agentic student learning and a collaborative teacher culture. By rethinking traditional practices and prioritising time for shared professional collaboration, schools can align their resources with their vision, toward regenerative growth and meaningful transformation.

Vision-led leadership: building culture with purpose

At the heart of transformative leadership is a compelling vision. This is not merely a statement of intent but a strategic catalyst, a vivid picture of a preferred future that energises people and aligns their efforts. When embraced collectively, vision provides the rationale for why change is necessary and the direction in which to head. It becomes the heartbeat of transformation, shaping how culture is cultivated and how practice is enacted.

The work of shaping a transforming culture begins with critically examining current values, both stated and lived. Misalignment between values and vision can stall progress or breed disappointment. When this gap is recognised, it presents an opportunity to refresh shared values and bring greater coherence to the lived experience of school life. This means that vision-led leadership is both relational and intentional, built on a foundation of trust and agency. Leading from this lens shifts from controlling to empowering, nurturing a culture where initiative and innovation are not only possible but expected.

Vision also functions as a decision-making filter. It offers clarity amid complexity and supports adaptability in a constantly changing environment. Leaders amplify its power by establishing enabling constraints by providing sufficient structure while simultaneously encouraging autonomy. This allows freedom to experiment, aligned with purpose, maintaining a consistent trajectory even when the path is non-linear.

Ultimately, it is the shared vision that holds the culture together. When culture is grounded in trust, collaboration, and a deep sense of shared purpose, the conditions are right for sustained innovation. Transformation doesn't happen because of vision alone, but without vision transformation lacks direction, energy, and coherence.

Yet vision, no matter how compelling, cannot live in the abstract. It must be enacted daily through routines, language, behaviours, and structures that reinforce alignment.

* * *

The next chapter explores *samepageness*. This is the disciplined practice of maintaining shared understanding and action. It is through this lens that schools move from aspiration to implementation.

Reflect and reimagine

1. **Think about a time when leadership empowered agency and collaboration:** What actions made this possible? or Where did leadership limit autonomy and innovation?
2. **How does your school's leadership structure currently operate?** What shifts in posture or practice could enable greater professional agency and shared ownership?
3. **How does your leadership team cultivate trust and collaboration?** What concrete actions could help create a culture where teachers feel safe to take risks and innovate?
4. **What assumptions about leadership or school structures need disrupting?** Which industrial-era practices may be holding back meaningful change?
5. **Imagine a distributed leadership model for your school:** What structures or behaviours would you prioritise – and what is one practical step you could take today?

Practical action

- **Decision-Making and Action-Taking** (p. 104): Help leaders and teams assess the nature of challenges they face, prioritise and sequence actions appropriately, and build confidence in navigating complexity by matching problems to the right strategic response.

- **Looking Back Across Generations** (p. 97): Help staff understand how their generational schooling experiences shape current beliefs and practices, using personal stories and the four elements to uncover assumptions and inspire more future-aligned learning environments.
- **The Leadership Charter** (p. 100): Co-create a shared charter that clarifies values, strengthens trust, and sets collective expectations for working together with coherence and purpose.
- **The One, The Few, The Many** (p. 102): Help leadership teams align personal purpose, team trust, and collective influence, to lead authentically.
- **Three Horizons Thinking** (p. 107): Map present realities, envision future aspirations, and identify strategic innovations by helping teams navigate complexity and plan purposeful transitions across short-, mid-, and long-term horizons.
- **Pulse Check:** Collaboratively assess your school's current reality across the four elements, creating a shared foundation for strategic planning and aligned action. Using the framing *What's working well?* and *Even Better if...*, analyse, critique, and suggest enhancement opportunities for the four elements:
    1. Learner experience (p. 123)
    2. Professional culture (p. 134)
    3. Management and systems (p. 151)
    4. Places, spaces, and resources (p. 171).

Learner Experience	Professional Culture	Management & Systems	Places, Spaces & Resources
What's working well?	What's working well?	What's working well?	What's working well?
Even better if...	Even better if...	Even better if...	Even better if...

Chapter 3
Samepageness: Building Alignment and Trust

Picture the back stage of a theatre, bustling with energy and purpose. The cast huddles, perfecting their lines, adjusting costumes, and aligning the details of their performance. They've spent weeks rehearsing for this moment. This private space is a sanctuary where mistakes are corrected, new ideas are tested, and trust is built. When the curtain rises, what unfolds on the front stage looks seamless – not just their skill, but the trust and preparation forged backstage.

From the back stage to the front stage

This theatrical picture provides a powerful metaphor for teams, drawing from Goffman's *The Presentation of Self in Everyday Life* (1959). He applies a dramaturgical model, likening social interactions to a theatrical performance:

- The **front stage** represents the public self we present to others.
- The **back stage** is where we are free to be ourselves, reflect, and prepare, away from external expectations.

In schools, the *front stage* is where teachers interact with students. In reality, it's more akin to avant-garde theatre with audience participation. The quality of this performance is shaped by the *backstage* work where co-teachers align goals, debate ideas, and negotiate roles. The back stage is a crucible for trust, shared understanding, and professional collegiality. Investing in these relationships lays the foundation for a seamless, unified presence.

This chapter explores the concept of being *on the same page*, developing what Goffman calls a *working consensus*, a shared understanding that enables teams and co-teachers to navigate the complexities of their front-stage 'performance'. By prioritising backstage collaboration, co-teaching teams can transform their practice, benefiting both teachers and students.

'On the same page'

As I talked to teachers in co-teaching contexts for my research, this stood out as a strong recurring theme, the secret sauce of success as they worked together in proximity. These settings demand more from teachers than simply adapting the practice used within a bounded, solo space. It requires a profound shift in how educators collaborate, communicate, and co-create. One teacher described this alignment when they said: 'We're on the same page – they can't play the mum versus the dad thing that kids do.'

This sentiment captures the essence of *samepageness*. Without it, co-teaching can feel chaotic, like rowing a boat with one person paddling left and the other right. And the result? Exhaustion, frustration, and little forward progress and then eventually a regression to the solo paradigm. But when alignment is achieved, collective efforts propel teams toward a shared vision, creating a seamless experience for students.

I have found that this alignment doesn't happen by accident. It's cultivated backstage by being intentionally collaborative and engaging in the informal strategic conversations. Teachers who embraced the back stage as a place to build trust, test ideas, and solve problems were professionally energised in these learning environments – a clear appreciation that 'we're all on the same page and we all know what's expected', as another teacher described it.

When co-teachers and teams establish a *working consensus*, this is evident in shared goals, clear expectations, and a united front as they work with their students. By prioritising this backstage collaboration, co-teachers can enhance not only their own professional satisfaction but also the quality of learning experiences they design for their students. As one teacher said:

> It's about finding a way to get on the same page with thinking and pedagogy, which takes time and effort but makes all the difference in how we work together. When we're not on the same page, it feels like we're pulling in different directions, and the students pick up on that.

I also spoke to teachers working in large multi-cohort learning spaces alongside colleagues, where it was not working optimally. One teacher's reflection went to the heart of the issue, encapsulating both the challenge and the untapped potential of alignment: 'Still wondering about the endless possibilities if both grade partners were on the same page.'

This comment was an important reminder. One teacher could see the potential for deeper learning, but their co-located (not co-teaching) colleague had other ideas. When backstage time wasn't prioritised, developing professional alignment became a struggle, and they found themselves out of sync with their team or frustrated by the missed opportunities.

Imagine if actors in a play had a quick chat about their roles as they walked from their dressing room to the stage, or even on the stage in front of the audience. *Samepageness* is not about making everyone teach the same way but creating a shared vision and understanding, drawing on strengths.

Distributed cognition: better together

The concept of *distributed cognition* was touched on in the introduction and will be developed a little more. It highlights that we think better together. Yet, the traditional, and seemingly prevailing model of schooling which reinforces individual cognition limits collaborative potential.

If we value student learning as connected and collaborative, this can be modelled and reinforced in teachers' work. *Samepageness* is the intentional alignment of vision, values, and practices. It becomes the mechanism by which distributed cognition is realised in the professional context, by supporting a trust-filled environment where collective intelligence enhances student outcomes and drives innovation.

Cognitive scientist Edwin Hutchins introduced *distributed cognition* in *Cognition in the Wild* (1995). He challenged the view of cognition as solely residing within the individual brain. Murphy Paul builds on this, illustrating how collaboration, shared tools, and collective problem-solving enhance thinking. Neuroscience research confirms that social interaction fosters richer thought processes than working alone.

This means co-teaching isn't just a preference or a nice-to-have; it's a scientifically supported method for enhancing teacher effectiveness and student learning by harnessing collective expertise.

Reaching *samepagenes*

Developing intentional alignment around a shared vision for the student experience isn't about enforcing uniformity but fostering coherence, appreciating difference, and working towards a consistent learning experience. It provides a practical application of distributed cognition, allowing individuals to leverage their collective strengths.

Samepageness involves three key elements:

1. **Shared vision** – A shared sense of purpose, establishing clear goals for student experience.
2. **Common values** – Guiding principles, ensuring alignment.
3. **Collegial practices** – Strategies and actions for teaching, management, and engagement, creating a cohesive professional culture.

A focus on these elements enables co-teaching teams to navigate the complexities of working together, maintaining flexibility with clarity and trust. It is the foundation that supports collaboration, enhances professional relationships, and elevates the learning experience for students.

It doesn't mean that individual co-teachers lose their professional identity. I have seen how it allows interests and passions to shine through within the team, as each works to their strengths.

Effective co-teaching

The foundation of successful co-teaching lies in alignment, ensuring that teachers work cohesively to enhance collaboration, design opportunities for deeper learning, and make space for introducing innovative ideas. In shared teaching spaces, where responsibilities are interconnected, a lack of alignment can lead to miscommunication, inefficiencies, and frustration. *Samepageness* mitigates these challenges by clarifying roles, building trust, and enhancing how we work. More than just streamlining collaboration, this alignment creates a unified front that directly benefits learners, providing them with a seamless and supportive learning experience.

I spent several years working at a K–12 school in Sydney led by Dr Stephen Harris, a pioneer in rethinking school culture, agentic learning, and spatial design. One of the most significant aspects of Stephen's leadership was disrupting the traditional solo-teacher model and empowering teachers to implement collaborative, team-based practice. A prime example of this vision was The Zone, a multi-cohort learning environment designed for 180 students in Grades 5 and 6, supported by six co-teachers.

The Zone went beyond an architectural innovation; it was a transformative approach to teaching and learning, where space, pedagogy, and collaboration worked in harmony. Purposefully designed spaces supported agentic, inquiry-based student learning, but the real power of The Zone lay in the culture and shared identity co-created by the team.

Behind the scenes, The Zone was defined by systems, routines, and rituals that fostered relational connectedness and a shared purpose among teachers. One critical practice was the co-creation of a *team agreement* at the start of the school year, which built trust and strengthened professional empathy, laying the foundation for sustained collaboration. This intentional alignment helped the teaching team develop the social capital necessary for their innovative practices to thrive, reinforcing the idea that strong professional relationships were mission-critical.

The Zone quickly became a beacon of innovative practice, annually attracting hundreds of visitors from across Australia and internationally. As visitors observed students deeply engaged in projects, they often remarked on the seamlessness and effectiveness of the learning environment. During one visit, a group member asked a student, 'When you have a problem, which teacher do you go to?' The student paused, looked around, and replied, 'Whoever's the closest.'

This simple response encapsulated the essence of The Zone's success as a shared, team-based approach where students felt equally supported by every teacher. It was a moment that captured the transformative potential of relational connectedness and collaboration – a testament to the co-teachers' significant backstage work.

For the students, their teachers' *samepageness* ensured consistency in expectations, teaching strategies, and support. When teachers operate from a shared understanding, they can deliver cohesive learning experiences, establish shared norms, provide targeted support for diverse needs, and use their time and expertise to greater effect. This seamless coordination strengthens the learning environment, making it more engaging, responsive, and impactful for all students.

Toward *samepageness*: practical strategies

Samepageness requires an intentional strategy. Co-teaching teams can foster alignment through structured collaboration, communication, and collective growth. I found that there were three critical elements for co-teachers' to reach *samepageness*:

1. **Create co-teaching agreements**
    - Establish shared vision and values, role clarity, and accountability.
    - Serve as a touchstone for navigating challenges and maintaining alignment.

2. **Dedicate time for reflection, review/critique, and iteration**
    - Regular structured conversations to celebrate successes, address challenges, and refine strategies.
    - Reflection tools, such as empathy mapping, to deepen understanding of learners.

3. **Intentionally build social capital**
    - Trust, respect, and psychological safety underpin effective co-teaching.
    - Investing in building authentic inter-personal connection and shared experiences strengthens these professional bonds.

As teams move toward *samepageness*, alignment becomes not just a goal but a natural outcome. Together, co-teachers create a vibrant, collaborative culture that enhances their professional satisfaction and the learning experiences of their students.

This is showbiz: the power of *samepageness* in action

At a secondary school renowned for its commitment to collaborative teaching and innovative learning environments, The Studio stood out as a model of co-teaching in action. Here, the music teaching team comprised Brett, a seasoned educator with over 20 years of experience, and Paul, an early-career teacher. Together, they demonstrated the transformative potential of *samepageness*. Brett and Paul reimagined the compulsory Year 8 music program, working in a refurbished space, purposefully designed to foster agentic collaborative learning.

The Studio was no ordinary bounded classroom. Two individual classrooms were merged to create a single multi-zoned learning environment with thoughtful furniture and fit-out. It included a large central space, the Green Room, for group collaboration, and around the perimeter were 'Jam Hubs' for rehearsal and fully equipped recording studios. This dynamic environment supported predominantly student-initiated learning within an inquiry approach, where the cohort of 57 students were grouped as 'bands' (seven or so students in each) engaged in deeper learning to compose, produce, and perform their own music. But it wasn't just the physical space that made The Studio exceptional, it was the intentional alignment between Brett and Paul that brought the learning environment to life.

Their shared vision was captured in a simple but powerful catchcry – 'This is showbiz' – a mantra that set the tone for their co-teaching practice, reminding both teachers and students that music was not just an academic subject to be taught but an immersive, creative experience. Their 75-minute sessions were carefully structured into rotations, with each teacher leading a different aspect of learning. Brett coached student bands on the Silent Stage, seamlessly integrating knowledge into performance. Simultaneously, Paul ran the Base Station, providing targeted feedback and teaching skills and required knowledge. In between, bands were working independently. This highly coordinated approach ensured every student received both structured instruction and the creative freedom to experiment.

Brett and Paul's *samepageness* was evident not just in their well-coordinated co-teaching, but also in their shared ethos, a commitment to students creating *something beautiful*. They were continuously refining their practice through regular reflection and iterative improvements, ensuring that their collaboration remained dynamic and responsive to student needs.

By modelling distributed responsibility and co-ownership, Brett and Paul created a seamless and engaging learning experience. On the *back stage*, their shared workflows included a centralised online portal for their planning and communication. On the *front stage* students experienced a cohesive, empowering journey through music. Brett and Paul demonstrated the power of relational connectedness and a shared commitment to agentic learning.

The Studio exemplifies how *samepageness* transforms teaching from an individual endeavour into a collaborative art. Through intentional alignment of vision, values, and practice, Brett and Paul cultivated a vibrant, future-focused learning community – one where creativity thrived and students were empowered to take ownership of their learning.

From alignment to agency

Samepageness fosters alignment, strengthens relationships, and creates a foundation for making progress into a purposeful future. Through intentional *back stage* collaboration, co-teachers enhance both professional satisfaction and student outcomes to build a culture of trust, coherence, and innovation.

But alignment is not the end goal; it lays the groundwork for what comes next: agentic learning design. When co-teachers are on the same page, they create the conditions for student agency to flourish. The clarity and cohesion developed through shared vision, values, and practice allow teaching teams to design learning that invites students to take ownership, make decisions, and engage deeply.

Just as co-teachers need *backstage* time to develop relational trust and unified purpose, students also need the *front stage* to reflect this alignment in the form of choice-rich, voice-enabled, and student-intitiated learning experiences. Without professional alignment, agency can feel unanchored or tokenistic. But with a united teaching team, student agency becomes purposeful, structured, and supported.

* * *

The next chapter explores how this foundation of *samepageness* enables co-teachers to design learning environments where students are not just participants but partners. It is here that the real shift occurs, from simply working together as educators to designing with intentionality for learner autonomy, inquiry, and growth.

Reflect and reimagine

1. **Think of a time when team alignment was strong.** How did it shape collaboration and trust? What happened when alignment was missing?
2. **What are the biggest barriers to co-teaching in your context?** How might distributed cognition and shared teaching improve learning?
3. **What structures could strengthen alignment and trust among teachers?** How might regular collaboration build a stronger sense of shared purpose?
4. **Which assumptions about teaching roles still limit collaboration?** What needs to shift to support shared ownership and co-creation?
5. **Imagine co-teaching is the norm in your school:** What agreements, principles, or systems would support alignment – and what's one step you could take today?

Practical action

- **Team Agreement** (p. 127): Co-teaching teams to build trust and alignment by co-creating a shared agreement that defines values, expectations, and working norms, laying the groundwork for sustainable, collaborative practice.
- **1-2-4-All: Purposeful Meetings** (p. 147): Ensure every voice is heard, supporting deeper thinking, shared insight, and equitable participation through a simple yet powerful process of reflection and collective synthesis.

Chapter 4
Agentic Learning Design

The Grade 3 co-teaching team consisted of five teachers working together in a shared learning space, creating a cohesive and dynamic environment for 90 students. Their space was designed for movement, flexibility, and agentic learning, but success required collective effort, adaptability, and trust.

The team understood that trial and error was not a sign of failure but an essential part of their journey. Each team member brought unique strengths, which they leveraged to iterate and refine their approach. Rory, one of the co-teachers, emphasised the importance of creating a culture of prototyping, testing small changes in spatial arrangements, learning activities, and student groupings, then debriefing as a team to evaluate the results.

During one backstage session, they reimagined their literacy rotations, integrating eight distinct activity stations. What would be difficult to manage for a solo teacher became possible with a unified team. Students flourished under the new structure, and the team continued to refine their approach as the term progressed.

By embracing an iterative process and leveraging each other's strengths, the Grade 3 team demonstrated how a culture of trust and collaboration can turn experimentation into sustained success.

In this chapter, we investigate designing for learner agency. We consider the structures, practices, and pedagogical choices that make space for student voice and decision-making. Agentic learning grows the capacity for students to be self-determined, resilient and purposeful learners, equipped not only to navigate complexity but to thrive in it.

Agentic learning

At the heart of *agentic learning* is the belief that learners are not passive recipients of knowledge, but active participants in their learning. It is a student's capacity to initiate learning work towards meaningful outcomes by amplifying their voice, choice, and ownership. Learners initiate: they are not merely doing what is required, but engaging with curiosity and purpose.

A learning environment that nurtures agency helps students to understand and appreciate the *why* behind what they are working on, to co-construct rich tasks and navigate pathways that align with their interests and goals, alongside the curriculum requirements. Autonomy is scaffolded, expectations are transparent, and learners are encouraged to develop their metacognitive awareness, self-regulation, and responsibility.

When we prioritise agency, it acknowledges that students bring experiences, perspectives, and capacities. They are not empty vessels waiting to be filled. Agentic learning design involves creating conditions for students to participate in shaping what and how they learn by engaging with authentic problems, working collaboratively, and reflecting on their progress. Learning is deeply personal and dynamic. Students' relationships with teachers become redefined, from those based on authority to becoming learners together, guides and motivators, exploring the world.

Learning design

Broadly speaking, *design* represents a problem-solving approach that is grounded in human-centred innovation. It has become a pivotal strategy for transformation in fields ranging from business and technology to healthcare and the social sector. It focuses on empathy (for the user), creativity (surfacing multiple ideas), and collaboration (distributed cognition). Design, as a thinking routine, fosters innovation aligned with the needs of the people it serves.

Successful businesses and public sector organisations have leveraged design principles to solve user problems and overcome barriers. Airbnb revolutionised the travel industry by deeply understanding user needs, refining its platform based on host and guest experiences, and building trust through high-quality property listings. Spotify redefined music consumption by personalising the listening experience, making an overwhelming catalogue easily navigable through data-driven curation. In the government sector, Service NSW improved their engagement with the public by streamlining digital and in-person interactions, reducing bureaucratic complexity, and designing service centres that prioritise people over process. The redesigned experience led to increased human interaction, reducing the digital interface.

Agentic learning design applies these same principles to the school experience, prioritising student ownership, autonomy, and active participation. Instead of passively receiving information, learner experience becomes the focus, and students are co-creators. Just as life-changing products and services emerge from deep user understanding, effective learning environments are shaped by deeply understanding the experiences, needs, and aspirations of students, the 'users'. By embedding design into educational practice, we can create learning environments that are innovative, adaptive, and truly responsive to learners.

From lesson planning to learning design

Reframing *lesson planning* as *learning design* reinforces a professional culture that moves beyond content delivery in a classroom towards understanding the interplay of people, pedagogy, and place to create an ecosystemic learning environment. While lesson planning follows a linear or mechanistic structure, learning design acknowledges the biologic complexity of the learning ecosystem, and the need for adaptability and responsiveness for student-initiated learning.

Planning assumes a predictable sequence of events, with pre-determined success outcomes. Agentic learning *design*, however, acknowledges that learning is influenced by:

- What piques a learner's interest
- How deeper learning is made possible
- Global, local, or contextual realities that can be explored to motivate learners
- The enabling constraints of the regulatory curriculum framework.

By shifting from rigid structures to a responsive design approach, educators empower students to actively shape their learning experiences, fostering deeper engagement and ownership. This does not, however, mitigate the importance of knowledge and skills learners require within a mandated curriculum. These perspectives are complementary to a holistic learning experience. This shift supports the goal of *deeper learning*, where understanding and application are prioritised, and knowledge is transferred across contexts.

Designing together: the power of collaboration

At the very heart of design is bringing people together around a problem that matters. The value of collective intelligence in complex problem-solving is critical. Hannah Critchlow (2019), in *Joined-Up Thinking: The Science of Collective Intelligence and Its Power to Change Our Lives*, like Annie Murphy Paul in *The Extended Mind*, underscores that our brains are wired for connection, and that when we work together, we generate more creative solutions than we would alone.

For more than a decade, I have facilitated collaborative design sessions with educators and professionals from other sectors. I've personally witnessed the value of shared tools to reach a working consensus. This has become an essential strategy for enabling voice and creating alignment. A collective framework is foundational to a team's *samepageness*, to reaching a shared understanding of purpose and direction. Without this, teams risk misalignment and fragmented thinking. By engaging in structured, iterative collaboration, we enhance our resilience, our creativity, and the quality of learning design. Co-teaching becomes a strategic practice that leverages diverse expertise to create richer, more impactful learning experiences.

The science of collective intelligence demonstrates that innovation flourishes in team settings. When we embrace this principle, we shift from working in isolation to designing dynamic, co-constructed learning environments that can respond to the complexities of our contemporary world.

The foundations of design

Design can be a catalyst to shift thinking. Planning presents a linear approach that is a subset of design, rather than a starting point. Design is iterative, dynamic, and can be deeply connected to improving the user experience.

IDEO's Tim Brown, in *Change by Design*, outlines five core stages of the design cycle. These stages can be applied to agentic learning design.

Change by design	Agentic learning design
Empathy	Understand student perspectives as user
Problem definition	Defining the challenge to engage all learners
Ideation	Generate creative solutions
Prototyping	Refine ideas into action, gain feedback and insight
Testing	Implement, observe, review, refine

A design-led process shifts the emphasis from content delivery toward a dynamic, student-centred focus that can incorporate a range of pedagogical approaches. Essentially, it applies abductive reasoning, drawing on both evidence-informed practice and the depth of experience across the team.

A design mindset embraces a way of thinking that encourages innovation, reflection, and the motivation to continuously improve the learning experiences for students. This cyclical approach supports the shift from only seeing the craft of teaching as a content delivery system to understanding the art of teaching as a dynamic, evolving design process, where both teachers and students actively shape the learning adventure. Central to the design mindset is seeing each learner as a unique individual.

Empathy in learning design

Empathy is the foundation of design. It helps us to focus our efforts on how 'users' (students) might experience learning that is deeper and meaningful to them. Developing empathy strengthens connection, belonging, and engagement by gaining a deeper understanding of individual need and motivation. Key questions guide empathic learning design:

- What matters most to these students?
- What barriers hinder learning, and how can these be addressed?
- What outputs sustain engagement and interest?
- Who are the outliers and how can we intentionally connect with them?

A disengaged student who struggles with traditional instruction may benefit from more hands-on, exploratory learning opportunities. An anxious student may require clearer scaffolding and predictable routines. Understanding these variations allows teachers to create responsive, student-driven learning environments that foster agency and engagement.

Empathy mapping

By investing time in exploring empathy by mapping student personas, we can design learning experiences that resonate with the real needs of diverse learners. Typically, a 'persona' does not represent one identifiable student, but is aggregated around a 'type' that epitomises particular interests or motivations. Students can see their experiences and input reflected in the design of learning.

Empathy mapping is a process of gaining a deeper understanding of how students think, feel, and engage with their environment. It provides a structured way to visualise student perspectives and ensure learning design meets their real needs rather than relying on our assumptions of what works and what interests students.

Usually, an empathy map gathers reflections or responses on:

- **What students say** – Their verbalised thoughts on learning and the experience of school.
- **What students think** – Internal reflections, goals, and concerns.
- **What students feel** – Emotional responses they express toward school and learning.
- **What students hear** – Comments from teachers, peers, and parents.
- **What students do** – Observable behaviours and engagement patterns.

Understanding student perspectives is critical to designing learner experiences. This forms the basis for learning design in structuring dynamic, adaptable, and agentic learning environments.

Empowering pedagogy through design

Janet sat with her arms crossed, her expression unreadable. Around her, a team of teachers exchanged wary glances, their reluctance evident in the silence that followed the principal's introduction. I was meeting the group for the first time. For years, they had discussed moving toward learning design, developing a student-centred approach, but every attempt at change had been met with resistance. Now, their principal, Marilyn, had engaged me as an outside facilitator for a three-day Design Engage workshop. Janet's frustration bubbled to the surface.

'We're just not ready for this,' she finally said.

Marilyn met her gaze, 'We've been talking about this for nine years,' she said. 'I think it's time.'

Over the three days, something shifted. The teachers explored student experiences through empathy mapping, identified barriers and opportunities they had previously overlooked, and engaged in problem-solving sessions. They applied a learning design scaffold, checking back on their student personas to ensure that their perspectives were considered. Finally, they looked at the classrooms, common areas, and resources to create a physical environment to support their learning design.

On our last day together, they were fully immersed, designing learning spaces with zones that prioritised student agency and collaboration. As the principal and I listened in, we noticed that Janet, once the most resistant, had become a vocal advocate for new ideas. What had begun as a reluctant exercise had transformed into a shared vision. She was ready at last.

Enabling constraints in learning design

'Design depends largely on constraints.' – Charles Eames, renowned designer, and architect

While an artist often works with the freedom to create purely for expression or exploration, a designer operates within constraints, balancing creativity with the practical demands of function, purpose, and context. We have already seen how enabling constraints are important for leading schools in complexity, setting clear parameters. The perspective now shifts to their place in the learning design.

Kites rise high against the wind, not with it.
CHURCHILL

In the dynamic environment of learning design, enabling constraints play a pivotal role. These boundaries provide structure to creativity, offering a balance between freedom and focus. Far from limiting innovation, enabling constraints act as guideposts, ensuring that the design process remains purposeful and aligned with internal and external requirements. Constraints challenge us to think critically and creatively, fostering more intentional and impactful outcomes.

Enabling constraints bring clarity by narrowing the field of possibilities. They focus energy on creating the conditions for learning design:

- Time constraints encourage us to prioritise what matters most.
- Curriculum guidelines provide a framework that can be used as a launchpad for deeper, interdisciplinary learning.
- Physical space limitations push educators to be inventive in maximising available resources for student engagement.

These constraints function as catalysts for experimentation, allowing us to stretch creativity within the curriculum, while staying connected to the constraints we all work within. This shared understanding enables co-teaching teams to align their efforts and work toward a common vision.

Constraints help to define the possibilities of learning design. Perceived constraints, such as rigid curriculum requirements, can either limit possibilities or serve as catalysts for creative solutions. Often, what seems unmovable may instead be an unchallenged assumption. Ask 'Is this still relevant?' or 'How might we...?' When questioning and reimagining boundaries, we can uncover hidden opportunities.

When effectively applied, enabling constraints inspire us to think outside the box while staying grounded in the realities of our context. Constraints are not barriers; they are design prompts that push learning experiences to be more intentional, innovative, and purpose-driven.

By shifting the perspective on constraints from restrictive to enabling, we move closer to designing meaningful, adaptable, and student-centred learning environments that prepare students for the complexities of the real world.

* * *

By embracing the role of designers, we create adaptive, student-centred experiences that align with the realities of contemporary education. Agentic learning design supports us to move beyond content delivery to co-create rich, responsive environments that prioritise ownership, engagement, and deeper learning. This shift calls for a new professional mindset, one that sees pedagogy not as a script to deliver, but as a dynamic, evolving experience to be designed.

Thoughtful design is amplified when the environment includes affordances that support deeper learning. Learning spaces are not neutral; they can enable or constrain pedagogical intentions. The next chapter explores the power of place, exploring how physical environments shape culture, influence behaviour, and act as the third teacher in learning. It examines how rethinking the design of learning spaces can amplify agentic pedagogies, support relational teaching, and better prepare students for the demands of our uncertain world.

Reflect and reimagine

1. **Think of a time when you were deeply engaged in learning:** What made it meaningful? How did autonomy or collaboration play a role?
2. **How might shifting from lesson planning to learning design support agency?** What would this change look like in your context?
3. **What practices could strengthen collaboration in your school?** How might shared tools (like empathy maps or design frameworks) support innovation?
4. **What assumptions about teaching need to shift to prioritise agency and empathy?** Which mindsets or routines might be getting in the way?
5. **Imagine a school designed for agentic learning:** What key principles or structures would support student ownership – and what's one step you could take today?

Practical action

- **Empathy Map** (p. 116): Step into the learner's perspective – develop rich personas that reveal students' lived experiences and guide the design of more inclusive, agency-rich learning environments.
- **Journey Map** (p. 120): Map the student experience to uncover disconnects, celebrate strengths, and generate clear, empathic priorities for a more intentional design.
- **Agentic Learning Design** (p. 130): Intentionally design learning experiences that are empathic, work within enabling constraints, allow for structured autonomy, and are grounded in real-work purpose.
- **Breaking Down Silos** (p. 145): Move beyond isolated practice by designing cross-disciplinary learning experiences that foster collaboration, curricular integration, and a more agile, connected school culture.

Chapter 5
The Power of Place: Rethinking Learning Spaces

The hum of 81 students filled the shared learning space as they moved seamlessly through different zones. With thoughtfully designed fit-out, writable surfaces, and flexible furniture, the environment enabled fluid movement and a variety of learning interactions. Four teachers navigated the space, guiding students through morning routines before moving into literacy rotations. While each teacher worked with a designated group, the space functioned as a cohesive ecosystem. Students were engaged in writing activities and independent work, and nearby a small group joined in a guided reading station with a parent volunteer. The learning support teacher worked closely with a small group nearby.

The co-teaching model reflected the flexibility of the space. Rather than working in isolation, the team operated as a collective unit, sharing responsibility for student growth. They adapted fluidly, stepping in as needed and supporting each other. As Toni noted, co-teaching alleviated the solo-classroom pressures, allowing teachers to collaborate and share fresh perspectives. More than just a teaching model, their partnership fostered trust, shared ownership, and professional wellbeing.

At the core of their practice was a commitment to preparing students for the future. 'The professional world isn't about working in isolation. It's about collaboration, problem-solving, and adaptability,' explained Ariana, one of the teachers. Their approach to pedagogy, space, and professional learning embodied this belief. They redefined structures, favouring fluid groupings over rigid divisions. Professional development was a collective effort, ensuring alignment in instructional language and practice. With proactive support from their principal, the team cultivated an environment where both students and teachers thrived. As they wrapped up the session and gathered for reflection, it was clear: this was more than a classroom, it was a community of learners built on trust, innovation, and a shared vision for the future.

Learning spaces are not merely physical containers; they are an embodiment of what matters. Re-imagining spatial design creates opportunities for diverse teaching and learning activities, fostering social connections and engagement in ways that traditional single-cell classrooms cannot.

While teachers have always adapted their environments, purposeful design shifts this from an incidental workaround to a strategic tool for transformation. However, space alone does not drive change; it is the alignment of spatial affordances with a professional culture that truly transforms a cool-looking design into a purposeful learning space.

This chapter explores the interplay between space, culture, and pedagogy, to leverage spatial design that enables deep learning, student agency, and collaboration. As we move beyond traditional classroom models, deliberate action is required to ensure that learning environments reflect and reinforce the values of a transforming school.

Growing spatial literacy

The shift from the traditional classroom construct to innovative spatial designs is not merely a physical change; it requires a fundamental shift in mindset and culture. The capacity to perceive, interpret, and respond to spatial affordances is a critical professional skill, often referred to as *spatial literacy* (Lackney, 2008).

Spatial literacy is a skill set that can be developed and refined over time – an evolving capacity to:

- Understand and respond to the relationship between pedagogy and space
- Recognise how the spatial affordances can enhance or limit certain activities
- Utilise affordances to identify and realise spatial potential
- Make strategic choices about how to arrange and use space to support diverse learner needs.

The idea that the environment actively shapes learning is well-established in educational philosophies. Reggio Emilia describes it as 'the third teacher' and Montessori as 'the prepared environment'. Both emphasise that thoughtfully designed learning spaces foster exploration, independence, and deep engagement.

The design mindset, notably in *The Third Teacher: 79 Ways You Can Use Design to Transform Teaching and Learning* (PWP/P Architects et al., 2010), reinforces the idea that learning spaces are not passive backdrops but become active contributors to effective learning. When we harness the power of space, we create environments that inspire collaboration, creativity, and student agency.

Spatial competence is a game-changer. Adaptive practitioners understand how physical space can be leveraged to support deeper engagement with learning. This skill is particularly critical for co-teachers during *backstage* time, including spatial dynamics in the design process to ensure a cohesive learning environment.

However, despite its importance, spatial competency often remains largely absent from pre-service teacher education. Programming might focus on lesson planning, curriculum scope and sequence, and behaviour management within the assumed context of a traditional classroom. Newly-minted teachers might enter the profession unprepared to navigate and optimise the spatial environment. Without explicit guidance, the default mindset often becomes unconsciously replicating their own school experiences.

To bridge this gap, both pre-service and in-service teacher education needs to:

- Introduce spatial literacy as an essential professional skill
- Provide opportunities for visits to diverse learning environments
- Engage with those experienced in optimising spaces for learning
- Encourage reflective practice on how spatial design influences student engagement
- Offer professional development focused on leveraging spatial affordances for innovative teaching.

By explicitly integrating spatial literacy into teacher education, both pre-service and in-service, schools can empower educators to confidently engage with non-traditional learning spaces. Rather than treating spatial design as a passive backdrop, we can actively shape and utilise space as a tool for deep learning, collaboration, and student agency.

Connecting learning design and spatial zones

Spatial literacy refers to the ability to understand how the physical arrangement of an environment influences behaviour, interactions, and learning outcomes. As traditional classroom boundaries are increasingly permeable, with operable walls and connections to adjacent and adaptive spaces, spatial literacy emerges as a critical skill.

This has both direct and indirect impacts on learning. Directly, the way spaces are arranged can either facilitate or constrain activities such as collaborative projects, independent study, and whole-group discussions. Indirectly, the environment communicates values and expectations. Spaces that prioritise openness and transparency can signal a culture of trust, empowerment, and shared responsibility, reinforcing pedagogical approaches that facilitate student-initiated learning.

The design of learning spaces plays a fundamental role in shaping teaching and learning practices. Dovey and Fisher (2014), from the University of Melbourne's Faculty of Architecture, identified a *continuum of spatial types* in schools, ranging from traditional closed classrooms to open-plan environments with adjoining spaces. Their research showed that spatial design is intrinsically linked to pedagogical intent. Imms et al. (2016) interpreted the Dovey and Fisher typologies by visualising physical environments and teacher practice as shown in the two diagrams opposite:

- **The spatial typology continuum** (top) maps learning-environment design, from the traditional bounded classroom to a completely open setting. In between, there are increasing levels of flexibility, permeability, and potential for ease of collaboration.
- **The pedagogical typologies** (bottom) depict a range of teacher–student configurations, moving from teacher-led to teacher-supported to student-initiated learning. These are not fixed roles, but fluid modes that reflect the growing involvement and agency of students.

Dovey and Fisher argue that traditional classrooms often reinforce hierarchical, teacher-directed instruction, limiting opportunities for student agency. In contrast, spatially responsive environments allow for more-dynamic interactions, supporting collaborative and student-centred pedagogies. When spaces are designed with intentionality, they not only accommodate a broader range of teaching strategies but also empower students to take greater ownership of their learning.

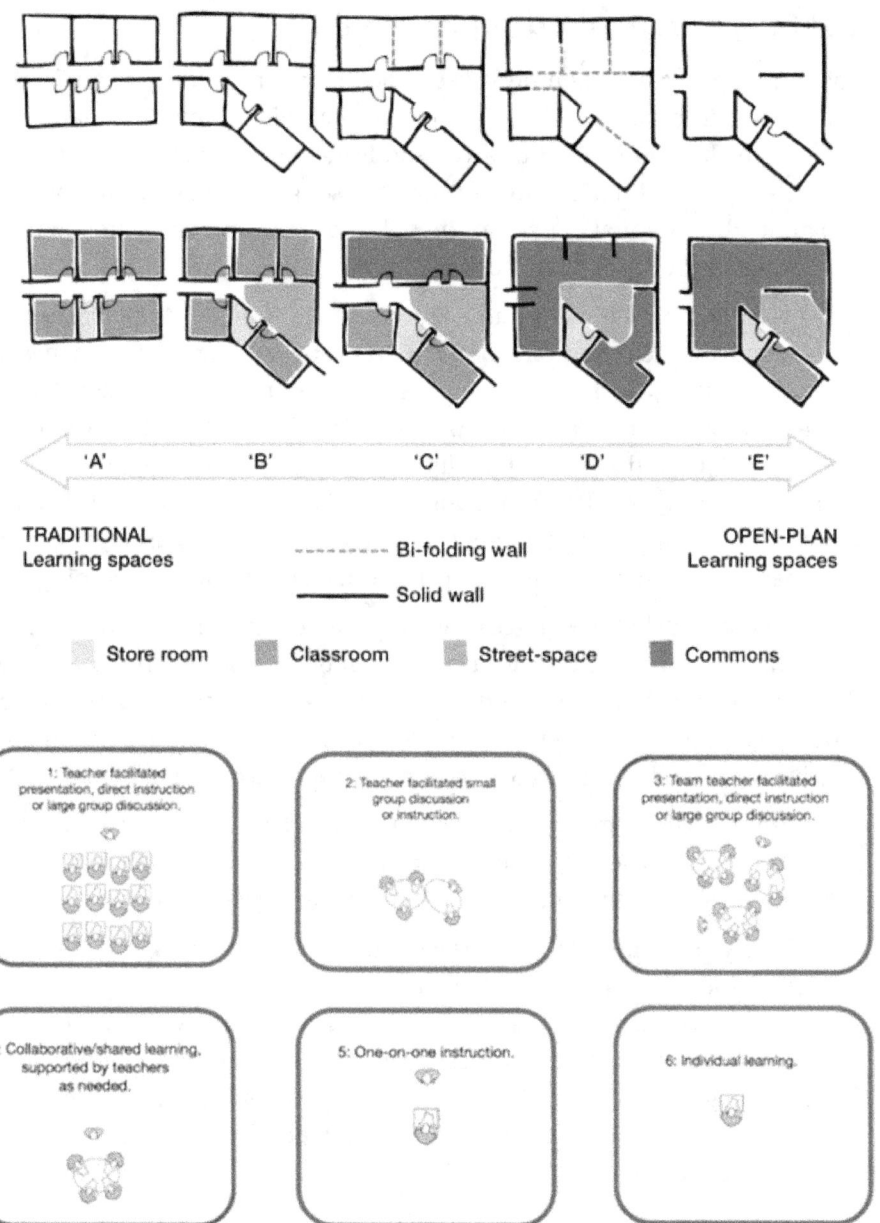

Dovey and Fisher's (2014) learning space types, as adapted in Imms, Cleveland, and Fisher (2016)

But first, a word about 'open plan'

The term 'open plan' often provokes strong reactions in discussions about learning environments and has become a catch-all for anything that is not a bounded classroom. On the Dovey and Fisher continuum, the open-plan example represents a design disruption that sought to break away from the constrained traditional classroom model. More recent design trends have advocated for the more nuanced spatial zoning approaches.

Schools that successfully integrate a more iterative approach to spatial design understand that learning environments are not a binary choice between 'open plan' and 'closed' classrooms. Instead, design decisions exist along a continuum of flexibility and intentionality. This is why Dovey and Fisher's typologies B, C, and D – which include breakout spaces, convertible classrooms, and multi-zoned environments – offer a more adaptable and effective framework for supporting the range of pedagogical modalities that encompass teacher-directed, teacher-supported and student-initiated learning.

The 'open plan' debate resurfaces regularly, often framed in overly simplistic terms that distract from the real issues. The reality is far more complex. Schools that embrace innovative spatial design are not rejecting structure but rather redefining it and creating environments that enable intentional, purposeful activity, which includes moving between different learning modalities.

For those of us working at the intersection of spatial design and pedagogy, the real conversation is no longer about open plan versus traditional classrooms. Schools that adopt a thoughtful posture to spatial design do so by:

- Aligning learning environments with their educational vision, rather than imposing a one-size-fits-all model
- Listening to teachers and students, hearing their perspectives, and recognising that different contexts require different spatial solutions
- Balancing structure and flexibility, allowing teachers autonomy to decide when to co-teach, when to work independently, and how to optimise space for diverse learning needs.

I regularly work with schools to develop design principles that seek to underpin learning environments that are flexible, intentional, and aligned with a shared vision for learning. This means moving beyond nostalgia, a desire to replicate the past, and instead focusing on creating environments that are focused on the future.

We are well past the point of debating whether learning spaces should evolve. The real conversation is about how we design environments that bring together the expertise of teachers and the agency of students.

Zoning for learning: designing spaces to support engagement

Creating effective learning environments for diverse approaches is not simply a case of removing walls but rather creating intentional zones that align with pedagogical goals.

David Thornburg (2004) introduced metaphors that have helped educators conceptualise learning spaces: *The Campfire*, *The Watering Hole*, and *The Cave*. These metaphors provide a framework for designing adaptive, agentic environments that support collaboration, deep learning, and creative expression.

- **The Campfire** – A space for storytelling, collective learning, and guided instruction.
- **The Watering Hole** – A space for informal, peer-to-peer collaboration and knowledge exchange.
- **The Cave** – A retreat for independent work, deep reflection, and self-regulation.

Broadening Thornburg's foundational metaphors, schools have developed and incorporated additional spatial zones that support different aspects of student engagement. These include:

The Workshop: spaces for making and inventing

Students explore ideas, create prototypes, and engage in hands-on learning.

- Equipped with tools, craft supplies, and digital-maker technologies.
- Encourages trial-and-error thinking through prototyping and iteration.
- Flexible layouts support collaboration, experimentation, and interdisciplinary projects.

The Mountaintop: spaces for presentation and vision

To showcase achievements, present ideas, and celebrate learning.

- **Focal points** such as stages or raised platforms encourage public speaking and pitching ideas.

- **Multi-modal integration** (microphones, projectors, digital screens) enhances visibility and accessibility.
- **Amphitheatre-style seating** provides a gathering space to learn together and share.

Outdoor Spaces: connection with nature

Access to nature significantly enhances cognitive function, focus, and wellbeing. In *Good Nature*, Kathy Willis (2024) highlights research showing that students with views of green space perform better on attention-based tasks than those facing a blank wall.

Schools that integrate biophilic design understand that human flourishing depends on connection to the natural world. Access outside provides:

- **Flexible learning areas** – Open-air classrooms with movable furniture.
- **Seamless indoor-outdoor transitions** – Covered areas that blend with indoor spaces.
- **Natural elements** – Gardens, trees, and water features that enhance focus.
- **Multi-sensory experiences** – Textures, sounds, and visuals that spark curiosity and engagement.

Empty Spaces: the power of minimalism and potential

Deliberate emptiness allows for flexibility, creativity, and movement. Unspecified areas invite experimentation, unstructured play, and self-directed learning.

- **Reconfigurable layouts** – Adaptable for ideation, prototyping, or movement-based learning.
- **Minimalist design** – Movable furniture and equipment that encourage flexibility.
- **Collaborative potential** – Modular tools such as writable panels and temporary partitions.

Rethinking learning spaces: a strategic approach

By integrating spatial zoning, we move beyond rigid, one-size-fits-all models toward environments that enable diverse learning experiences. Thoughtful spatial design ensures that learning spaces are not passive backdrops but active participants in shaping engagement, collaboration, and student agency.

Evaluating the impact of spatial design

Spatial design is not a set-and-forget process. Like learning design, it requires ongoing observation, reflection, and evaluation to ensure alignment with pedagogical goals and support of the social and emotional context. We continuously observe and assess whether spaces effectively support our pedagogical and social aspirations.

To evaluate the impact of spatial design, a range of evaluative strategies can be applied:

- **Structured observation** – Monitoring how students and teachers use the space throughout the day to identify patterns, points of friction, and opportunities for improvement.
- **Feedback cycles** – Gathering insights from students and teachers, and finding out what's working well and what adjustments are needed.
- **Learning outcomes analysis** – Assessing changes in engagement, collaboration, and academic performance linked to specific spatial modifications.

By treating spatial design as an evolving process, schools can ensure that learning environments remain responsive, purposeful, and aligned with educational goals. The spatial typologies diagram below provides a visual language to support teams in zoning learning spaces intentionally.

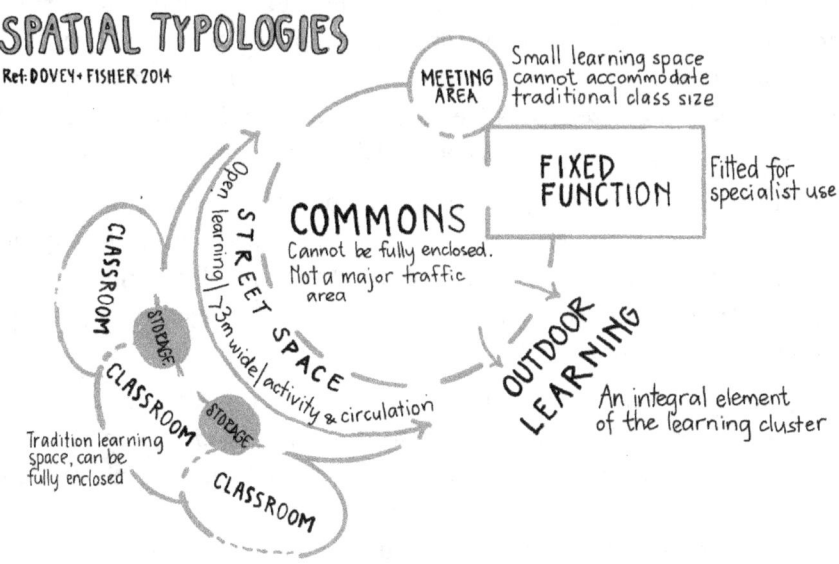

The visual analysis (diagram) draws on Dovey and Fisher's typology and provides a practical lens through which to consider the diverse functions and affordances of spaces for learning. When thoughtfully combined, sub-spaces create a flexible and responsive environment that supports a wide range of pedagogical approaches. I have observed successful practice when a combination of elements are incorporated into the spatial design:

- **Classroom/teaching space** – Bounded space, with/without operable walls between. Broad doorway openings can provide access to adjacent street space, commons, or breakout options.
- **Street space** – Connected to learning spaces/bounded learning spaces/classrooms. More than a corridor, it can be used for breakout and circulation (minimum 3 metres wide).
- **Commons** – A central gathering space for multi-cohorts; a place for group or individual work, with visibility/lines of sight.
- **Meeting area** – Smaller spaces for focused group work or small group teaching.
- **Fixed function** – Specialist areas, such as maker, labs, or studios.
- **Outdoor learning** – Intentional learning area connected to nature and screening/sun-safe factors.

Taken together, these spatial elements invite us to think holistically about the learning ecosystem.

Diversity in spatial design begins with architectural variety, then extends the possibilities for learning by allowing for movement, choice, visibility, and adaptability. This intentional layering of space empowers us to design experiences that are collaborative, differentiated, and deeply aligned with the needs and aspirations of learners and their teachers.

Spatial design is more than just a backdrop for learning; it is an active agent that shapes experiences, fosters collaboration, and enhances student agency. Taking the step – or leap! – to move beyond traditional classroom models requires intentional design that aligns with vision, pedagogical aspirations, and social connection.

The provision of space alone does not drive human transformation. True innovation occurs when spatial affordances are purposefully aligned with a school's vision and the complementary professional culture. This demands a commitment to growing spatial literacy, developing our ability to interpret, adapt, and optimise learning environments to support diverse student needs. Schools that embrace intentional spatial design create conditions for deeper learning and student-initiated exploration that is underpinned by learning that is both teacher-led and teacher-supported.

This begins with visionary leadership by those willing to rethink the default design of schools to create environments that truly support how students learn best and how teachers grow their professional practice. It means the places, spaces, and resources actively shape engagement, agency, and the culture of learning. Schools that approach spatial design with intentionality and adaptability can cultivate the skills, mindsets, and collaborative cultures needed for the future.

* * *

Part 1 has established foundational principles. Part 2 turns these into action. It offers practical tools, frameworks, and activities that bring these concepts to life. It is designed to support you to navigate transformation, whether initiating change or deepening existing practice. By engaging with these resources, you can begin to intentionally shape your spatial environments. The journey continues with practical steps that make innovation tangible, grounded, and most importantly, sustainable.

Reflect and reimagine

1. **Reflect on a learning space you've taught or learned in:**
   How did it affect engagement, collaboration, or agency? Did the space enable or limit learning?
2. **How well does your current environment support diverse learning approaches?**
   What small spatial changes could enhance flexibility or functionality?
3. **What training have you had in spatial literacy?**
   How might professional learning help you use your space more intentionally?
4. **Which assumptions about classroom design still shape your school?**
   What needs to shift to support adaptive, student-centred spaces?
5. **Imagine a transformed learning environment:**
   What zones, features, or principles would you prioritise and what's one change you could make today?

Practical action

- **Spatial Design Principles** (p. 162): Co-create clear, values-driven spatial design principles that align with their educational vision – empowering them to shape learning environments with purpose and confidence.
- **Amplifying Spatial Literacy** (p. 159): Deepens educators' understanding of how physical spaces shape learning and empowers them to design environments that intentionally align with pedagogical purpose, values, and human experience.
- **Affordances A–Z** (p. 165): Explore how physical spaces invite specific behaviours, using affordances as a lens to collaboratively design learning environments that are inclusive, intentional, and aligned with pedagogical purpose.
- **Designing for Future Learner Experience** (p. 168): Engage in reflection, analysis, and site-based observation to align pedagogy and space with a clear, future-focused vision for learner experience.

Part 2
The Playbook

Chapter 6
From Theory to Action

Part 1 introduced the core concepts that emerged from my work with schools and research for my PhD thesis. It lays a foundation for understanding what is needed to shift toward transforming schools for the future. The Playbook is a practical resource designed to help you navigate complex topics with actionable tools and structured frameworks. It serves as a companion for implementation, offering guidance, strategies, and reflection points that support real-world application.

The Playbook is:

- Practical and action-oriented, designed for direct use in the field
- Framework-driven, with structured tools for assessing, planning, and implementing meaningful change
- Interactive and reflective, encouraging active engagement through discussion questions and action steps
- Navigational, helping leaders orient themselves within a complex process and guiding them step by step toward transformation.

It supports the development of a strategic journey that aligns culture, pedagogy, systems, and places to move toward this vision, and provides guidance on taking action and sustaining change by embedding transformation into professional culture.

The tools in the Playbook will help to assess your current reality by examining existing practices, surfacing unexamined assumptions, and questioning long-held traditions. As team-based processes, the shared outputs help to foster clarity in transforming school within your unique context, as collegial routine, drawing on distributed cognition.

On the back stage: tools for strategy and decision-making

In Chapter 3, I introduced the analogy of the theatre, where the front stage is seen as the public-facing performance of professional practice, while the back stage is where we build alignment, trust, and coherence. I used Goffman's dramaturgical metaphor to explain that the quality of what unfolds in learning environments is shaped by the depth of preparation, reflection, and conversation that take place away from our work with students. Without this intentional behind-the-scenes collaboration, teacher teams can risk fragmentation, confusion, and fatigue.

The private rehearsal space, honing the performance, building trust.

The public-facing performance, the result of all the work, passion & dedication

The tools in Part 2 are designed to support the essential *backstage* processes that underpin future-focused, collaborative practice. These frameworks, protocols, and reflection guides are not just operational checklists, but are catalysts for conversation, designed to support decision-making and action-taking through collaborative and strategic lenses. They enable teams to align vision, values, and practices – *samepageness* – so that what happens on the *front stage* is seamless and purposeful.

Backstage work is a non-negotiable part of professional practice essential to outworking the vision of a transforming school. A strong *backstage* culture makes our complex work not only possible, but energising. As one teacher commented to me, 'It's not about being the same; it's about knowing what we're doing and why we're doing it – together.' The Playbook equips teams to workshop and rehearse their strategy before the curtain rises.

How to use the Playbook

This is not a step-by-step map with a fixed starting point or a set destination. Transformation is not a straight path from point A to point B. Instead, the Playbook serves as a compass, helping you to survey the landscape, identify your starting point, and navigate toward your unique vision for the future. On this adventure you will be encouraged to:

- **Assess the current reality** – Where are we now? What foundations have shaped our school?
- **Clarify the vision for the future** – What do our students need from us? How do we define future-ready?
- **Decide with boldness** – Where are we headed and what are we prepared to keep, ditch, tweak, renew and transform?
- **Use frameworks and tools for action** – Scaffolds that keep dialogue and strategy on track.
- **Support ongoing reflection and iteration** – This might be the beginning, but there is rarely an end point. How do we sustain change and continue to adapt?

You are invited to explore the sections that are most relevant to your school's vision for the future, revisit concepts as needed, and adapt strategies to fit your community.

This is important: a culture of shared decision-making

If we believe the values of learning include concepts such as agency, engagement, connectedness, and collaboration, then the professional culture in our schools can evolve to reflect these principles. *Samepageness*, the intentional alignment of vision, values, and practices, becomes the mechanism by which shared ownership of the strategic vision can be realised. More than simply working together or planning a task list, it is about creating a cohesive, trust-filled environment where the *distributed cognition* enhances shared outcomes and drives innovative practices.

Navigating the complexity of our world demands that our collective intelligence must be harnessed in a world where 'information is abundant, expertise is specialised, and issues are complex' (Annie Murphy Paul,

The Extended Mind). It reminds us that learning and ideas are no longer limited to siloed authority or top-down commands, orders issued from on high, but extend across people, tools, and environments. While leadership retains the responsibility, the quality of the decision-making can be enhanced by listening, observing, and consulting broadly.

Why use collaborative tools for shared decision-making?

The science behind distributed cognition reveals that collaboration taps into the brain's social nature, enhancing creativity, decision-making, and problem-solving. We know from advances in neuroscience that group interactions activate diverse areas of the brain, fostering richer and more complex thought processes than can be achieved by working alone.

In *The Extended Mind*, Annie Murphy Paul draws on the research by Gary and Judith Olson on the value of shared artefacts: 'One major contributor to success of group cognition... is the effective use of shared artefacts, which are ideally large, complex, persistent and revisable' (p. 234).

The Olsons concluded that such shared tools were essential for *samepageness*, or as they described it, 'singing from the same sheet of music'. Such complex artefacts allow the thinking of the group to be explicit. Such tools are most effective when they are 'preserved, retained and kept continuously visible – but also revisable'. Hence the value of the 'war room' (more to come on that).

In educational contexts, this means that including diverse voices in decision-making is not just a matter of preference but an evidence-supported method for improving both teacher effectiveness and student learning.

To harness the benefits of distributed cognition, collaborative tools are presented and explained throughout this Playbook. These tools are designed to:

- Facilitate structured dialogue that supports meaningful discussions
- Ensure transparency in decision-making, aligning teams with shared goals and values
- Collect data, ideas, and feedback from a range of voices
- Promote coherence and consistency, building a collective understanding of shared practices
- Encourage adaptive problem-solving, providing mechanisms for teams to reflect, iterate, and refine their approaches
- Provide a means for diverse voices to be heard.

Integrating collaborative tools provides practical ways for teams to engage in shared decision-making that is intentional, informed, and impactful.

A suite of tools

Over the last decade, I have developed tools and drawn on the expertise of others who work this way. In 2019, I had the opportunity to attend a three-day workshop on *Liberating Structures*, a suite of tools that harness all voices for shared decision-making, led by one of its co-creators, Keith McCandless. His approach demonstrated the power of structured, inclusive tools for fostering collaboration.

This experience showed me the value of making space for meaningful dialogue in workshops and meetings. Often, when I'm trying to wrap up a session, there's pushback: 'We just never have the time to talk about these important things during our time at school.' Tools scaffold dialogue and help people to stay on track and reach a working consensus around a shared problem.

As I facilitate workshops, large and small, I am particularly conscious of the quieter, more reflective participants. The contributions of these people can be deeply thought-through and are invaluable. Often, they remain unheard during a vibrant discussion with more dominant contributors. Providing time for groups to think before discussing is critical, as is finding ways for individual responses to be gathered. As I have often discovered, the quiet ones usually bring the gold.

Over years of working in this way, I've found that the right tools don't just structure conversations; they also unlock them. When used intentionally, the right tools create the conditions for clarity, collaboration, and commitment. As a facilitator, my role is to create space where every voice is heard and every contribution matters, especially those that might otherwise go unnoticed. The tools presented in the Playbook are invitations to reflect, to connect, and to move forward together with shared purpose. Whether guiding a large system-wide initiative or a focused team workshop, I've seen how structured dialogue can shift culture, spark innovation, and build momentum for meaningful change.

Reaching *samepageness*

The intentional alignment of teams around a shared framework of vision, values, and practices is not about enforcing uniformity but fostering coherence, appreciating difference, and working towards agreement, with a sense of optimism. This approach allows teams to leverage their collective strengths while ensuring a consistent and unified experience for students.

Samepageness as a meta-principle involves alignment in three key ways:

- **Shared vision:** Working together to establish clear goals for student learning, creating a shared sense of purpose and direction.
- **Common values:** Upholding shared principles that guide decisions and interactions.
- **Aligned practice:** Reaching agreement on ways of working and developing a positive culture.

Focusing on these elements enables teams to navigate the complexities of working together with flexibility, clarity, and trust. It serves as the foundation for collaboration, enhances professional relationships, and ultimately elevates the learning experience for students.

As you engage with this Playbook, the collaborative tools can help you in reaching *samepageness* with your teams and colleagues, ensuring that decision-making is shared, strategic, and future-ready.

Preparing for transformation: creating a 'war room'

A *war room* can be a dedicated place or even a space (like a wall) designed to centralise and organise your thinking. It has been used for creative, strategic, and collaborative activity in business and innovative industries. Displaying artefacts helps to visualise thinking, map connections, and refine strategies in real-time.

The war room is more than a meeting room with whiteboards and sticky notes, but a dynamic environment for problem-solving and decision-making, where ideas evolve, and clarity emerges through shared focus and interaction.

I first came across this way of visualising strategy and progress when I visited an architecture studio, at the beginning of my curiosity about school spatial design, more than 15 years ago. I was intrigued by how one large wall in a public space showed the elements of a school design project, with red string *linking concepts and annotated notes expanding on each step.* This wasn't tucked away somewhere but provided an opportunity for the teams to ponder and reflect with a cup of coffee in hand.

It can be invaluable for teams working on transformational initiatives. By mapping out frameworks, timelines, challenges, and solutions in one shared space, we can see the 'big picture' while simultaneously addressing the finer details. This space encourages iterative thinking, deep collaboration, and shared ownership of goals. Whether it's used for strategic planning, growing professional culture, or re-imagining learning environments, the concept of a *war room* supports teams in making their thinking visible, encouraging reflection, and driving actionable outcomes. It becomes a space where ideas are generated and captured, refined, and translated into meaningful action. Many of the tools in the Playbook can form the artefacts for the war room, creating a shared narrative and being a catalyst for meaningful change.

The foundations of transformation: Senge's iceberg

Peter Senge is a globally recognised thought leader in organisational learning. He introduced systems thinking as a foundational discipline for organisations seeking deep, sustainable change in *The Fifth Discipline: The Art and Practice of the Learning Organization* (1990). Senge's work highlights the importance of mental models, shared vision, and team learning, laying the groundwork for strategic transformation through cultural and systemic alignment.

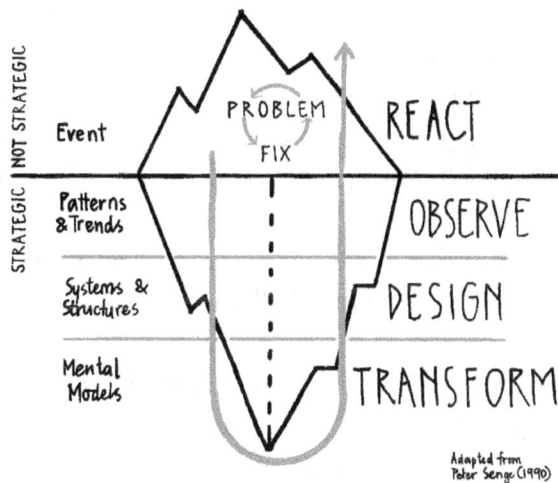

Too often, we find ourselves trapped in a problem-solving loop, reacting to visible events without addressing the deeper structures that shape them. Senge's Iceberg encourages us to look beneath the surface: to identify patterns, uncover systemic structures, and challenge the mental models that reinforce the status quo. This playbook builds on that foundation. Each section is designed to guide you through the layers of transformation and helps you to move from isolated fixes to holistic redesign. By drawing on the elements of learner experience, culture, systems, and space, we apply the Iceberg's depth-thinking to the very fabric of school life.

In any complex system, the surface activity is rarely the whole story. We naturally focus on headlines in front of us – these might be test or exam results, attendance rates, behaviours, or crisis points, and it is tempting to just try to 'fix'. What lies beneath the surface of an event shapes what happens above it. These submerged layers are where transformation truly begins.

Lasting change, beyond the problem-fix loop, means a shift in how people think, relate, and organise. This is where strategy becomes more than a document on the shelf. Senge reminds us that strategic thinking is linked to observing, designing, and transforming by:

- Looking for the patterns in the problems
- Designing new systems
- Challenging mental models
- Shaping an aligned culture.

This means we are working *on* the culture, not just *in* the system. It's why this Playbook reinforces *samepageness*, through developing common language and collective ownership. These are not as soft extras, but the unseen anchors of strategy that endure.

As you move through the four elements that follow – learner experience, professional culture, management and systems, and places, spaces, and resources – keep asking:

- Are we reacting to symptoms or addressing root causes?
- Are we brave enough to see what's really lurking beneath the surface?

The four elements of transforming school

We can reframe the experience of school as dynamic ecosystems where learners, educators, systems, and environments interact in constantly evolving ways. Transformation within such complexity cannot happen in silos. Instead, it requires a holistic framework that honours the interdependence of the system's parts. This Playbook is grounded in that premise.

I was first introduced to this concept through a quote in the foundational reading for my PhD that has stayed with me: 'School design should be viewed as a network of elements that together shape the learning environment' (Gislason, 2010).

The idea that a school operates as a living system of interconnected elements resonated deeply. Gislason's original framing of ecology, organisation, culture, and milieu provided a conceptual map. In this Playbook, I've reshaped these elements into the four interconnected elements that speak more directly to the lived reality of schools:

1. Learner experience
2. Professional culture
3. Management and systems
4. Places, spaces, and resources.

As explored in Part 1, each of these elements interacts with and influences the others. Change in one element ripples across the entire system. When aligned, the elements reinforce one another, creating the conditions for sustained transformation. When disconnected, they can produce friction, fragmentation, and even inertia as separate siloes.

Driving this model is vision, giving purpose to *learner experience* and serving as a compass that guides decisions across all elements. Without this anchor, change efforts risk becoming scattered and superficial.

A thriving *professional culture* supports innovation, growth, and connectedness. It's where relational trust, collaboration, and continuous professional learning allow new practices to take root. But culture does not emerge in a vacuum; it is sustained (or undermined) by the systems that scaffold it and shaped by the prevailing values that guide decisions.

Management and systems are often invisible but deeply influential. Organisational charts, managing structures, resource allocation, timetables, and decision-making protocols form the infrastructure that either enables or constrains transformation. These systems can be intentionally designed to reflect the priorities of the learner experience and promote human connection.

Finally, *places, spaces, and resources* are the tangible (physical and material) expressions of a school's values. When thoughtfully designed, they amplify agency, collaboration, and wellbeing. But even the most beautiful spaces fall short when disconnected from the systems, culture, and vision they are intended to support.

Together, these four elements form the school ecosystem, providing a useful framework to work through the core elements of a school. This Playbook is your guide for navigating that landscape. As you read, reflect on where you are now, what shifts are needed, and where you aspire to go. Your path will be unique, but these elements provide the scaffolding to help you move forward strategically, coherently, and with purpose.

Have you noticed?

This framework echoes Simon Sinek's *Start with Why* (2011), beginning with purpose, then moving to process (human and system), and finally product (space). In my work with schools, I often observe a well-intentioned leap straight to *what*, focusing on the physical environment or a new shiny tech-tool. I've heard it said, 'We just need sofas and a coffee table n the shared space', without a clearly articulated *why* or a coherent *how*. Strategic design that begins with *why* develops a shared *how*, and then considers the *what*. When all elements are aligned, a foundation for lasting transformation can be built. It may feel slower at first, but the long-term impact is more sustainable, adaptable, and meaningful.

These elements are a living network. Change in one impacts another. For example:

- A timetable adjustment (system) can support opportunities for co-design (culture), which influences the design of a learning commons (space) and ultimately improves student agency (learner experience).
- A wellbeing initiative in learner experience may require new staff practices (culture), different allocation of roles (systems), and quieter, restorative spaces (places).

When strategic decisions consider all four elements as part of a unified whole, change becomes more coherent, more sustainable, and more human.

From framework to action

Understanding the school ecosystem is only the beginning. The real work lies in translating these insights into deliberate, strategic action. Each of the four elements – learner experience, professional culture, management and systems, and places, spaces, and resources – will be unpacked in detail, grounded in the principles explored so far.

To support you in taking meaningful steps, each of the remaining chapters concludes with *practical action* tools. These tools are designed to support focused reflection, conversation, and prototyping ideas with your team. Whether you're at the beginning of your transformation journey or deep into it, the tools will help you assess your current reality, identify leverage points, and move with purpose toward your vision.

The goal is not a fixed destination, but continuously seeking alignment. Let these actions be the stepping stones, anchored in your context, shaped by your people, and fuelled by a clear and compelling vision for the future of learning.

Chapter 7

Transforming Leaders: Laying the Foundation

What must be in place before transformation can occur? The key to leading schools with a transforming vision is balancing accountability and responsibility with agency and empowerment and lessening top-down directives.

The core message from Part 1 is the need to have the courage to challenge long-held assumptions about school. Across generations we have replicated the same systems, followed the same structures, and assumed they are unchangeable. It's time to challenge these assumptions and think differently, to become transforming. When assumptions are challenged, what action is taken?

Why this matters

Think about building a house: it's more than just bricks and mortar, it's a home for a family. The architect observes and listens, then creates a plan that meets the current and future needs of the people who will live there. They consider how many adults will be living there, the children, their ages, and how the home might be adaptable over time. Some envision a 'forever home,' while others see it as a five-to-ten-year stepping stone. No matter the plan, the design is personal, and one thing is certain: just like designing a home, building a school culture begins with a solid foundation.

In the same way, transforming schools are not created by accident, nor will they appear through maintaining a business-as-usual approach. Transforming a learning culture requires intentional design, beginning with leaders who are willing to break the mould and establish a strategic foundation. Schools that successfully navigate transformation recognise that sustainable culture change follows vision-led strategy. Without a co-created and future-oriented strategic foresight, efforts to shift culture and pedagogy, and to enhance learner experience, are likely to stall.

This section focuses on the two foundational pillars that need to be in place before meaningful transformation can occur:
- Creating alignment
- Taking action.

When these elements are established, they create the structural integrity for a school's culture, pedagogy, and student experience to evolve in alignment with its vision.

From theory to action

The four elements provide a helpful lens to think strategically about each aspect of transformation. While each domain is interconnected, I approach them in a way that highlights the human aspects over the non-human, with learner experience as the first priority, followed by the complementary professional culture, and the organisational and spatial elements last.

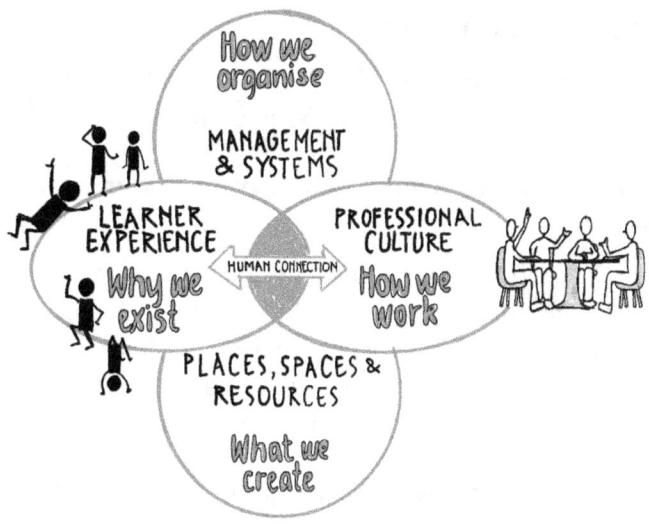

Human elements

Schools are for people, where students and staff can thrive and flourish.

Why we exist: vision and mission that are taking us somewhere

Our priority is *learner experience*, the foundation of a school's *why*. It represents the vision, focused on creating a learning, social and wellbeing context that articulates what we seek to achieve for our students. The success of making progress toward the vision relies significantly on the culture and the values that are embodied and modelled by the staff to enable the learner experience.

How we will work: shared values that guide decisions and actions

Situated in the *professional culture* domain, the quality of the collegial relationships across the school is pivotal to the aspiration for learner experience. This can only be achieved through an intentional focus on growing and shaping a complementary staff culture.

Learner experience and *professional culture* represent the human factors and are always the starting point for developing a strategic pathway for the future. The next two elements represent the non-human aspects, which must always serve the human connection, rather than being stand-alone siloes, disconnected from purpose.

Non-human elements

The way we organise and plan from a transformational perspective provides the fuel for the vision and mission to get to where they need to go.

How we will organise: operational systems and structures that enable

When we think about *management and systems*, we know that schools need to be efficiently run, well-organised and fiscally responsible. Operational systems and decisions are designed to serve the vision. Too often systems and structures remain untouched in the name of efficiency and sailing a steady ship (perhaps even keeping in the safe harbour).

What we create: physical environment and material resources

With the tangible and visual nature of *places, spaces, and resources*, it can be tempting to leap to the physical aspects first, especially when deadlines are looming. But if the human foundations are solid, and we have clarity on the organisational elements, then the physical design and fit-out are likely to be more lasting and adaptable to our needs.

Strategic alignment and action

Thoughtful strategic design can position us in powerful ways. It can:

- **Signal to the world that we are bold enough to think differently** for current and future generations of learners by offering an optimistic vision that sees their future as abundant with untapped possibilities.
- **Cultivate a workplace culture that is human-centred and community-driven,** a culture that stretches capabilities, grows collective capacity, and becomes magnetic in attracting and retaining great people.

This is why laying the foundation is critical. When strategy begins with clarity of purpose and is anchored in culture, it creates a cohesive throughline from vision to systems, to resource allocation, to buildings. Every operational decision becomes an expression of your aspirational identity.

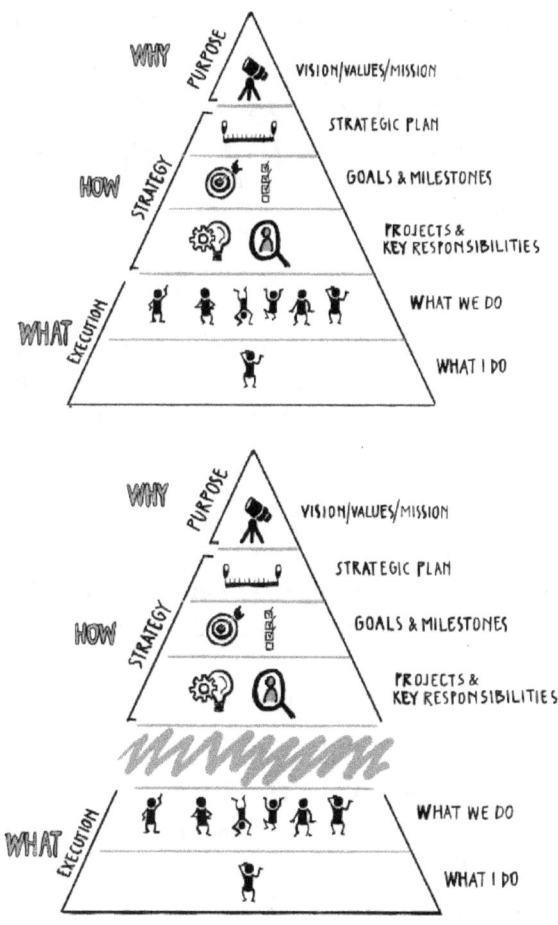

Yet too often I've seen schools articulate a compelling vision, only to encounter a disconnect between the lofty aspirations of strategic plans and the lived experience of their people. Between *why* and *how*, and then *what*, a gap emerges, where day-to-day operations fall out of step with longer-term intent. This misalignment weakens momentum, making it difficult to enact meaningful change that lives beyond the pages of a beautifully crafted strategy plan.

To shape a transforming school, strategic plans move beyond rhetoric and into the lived reality. A tangible alignment between vision, values, systems, and resourcing is made. Emerging projects in a strategic plan will impact professional culture. Where maintenance or business-as-usual gives way to building something for the future, people need reassurance that they will be supported through the strategic transformation. Clear and consistent communication, however challenging the process might be, is essential.

Articulating a vision, one that clearly prioritises what matters most to your community and that resonates across its breadth, is key. From this vision, aligned values provide the compass for decisions and behaviours, ensuring that daily practice is anchored in shared beliefs.

But a compelling vision alone is not enough. It must be supported by robust systems and structures that enable its enactment. These include leadership pathways, team (re)organisation, re-designed learning architecture, and feedback mechanisms. Crucially, resourcing decisions – how time, people, and funding are allocated – must align with the strategic direction. When these elements work in concert, the strategy moves from being a document to becoming a lived reality.

As you reflect on your strategic plan, consider the following questions:

- Is there alignment with your vision?
- Do your existing school policies, funding models, and professional learning structures reinforce traditional or future-oriented culture and practice?
- What is one structural shift that might bring your plan closer into alignment with your vision?

These questions lay the groundwork for identifying where misalignment may be holding you back from making progress toward the vision. They point to the critical role of leadership in making the strategy real. In this context, leadership is about having the people and practices in place to lead change courageously, consistently, and collaboratively.

Growing an aligned culture

How do we embody the culture we aspire to create? Great leaders are no longer defined by hierarchy or control, but by influence, vision, and service. It is the leader's mindset and behaviour that signal what is valued, shaping the conditions in which others can thrive.

Transformational leaders are:

- **Adaptive** – Embracing complexity with confidence, not seeking to control every variable, but learning in real time, responding with curiosity, and pivoting with intention.
- **Collaborative** – Moving away from top-down authority toward shared leadership models, where responsibility and insight are distributed across teams and individuals.
- **Visionary yet practical** – Holding the long view while grounding aspirations in everyday actions, ensuring that the strategic vision is living, not just a laminated poster.
- **Connected and empathic** – Deeply attuned to the needs, stories, and aspirations of the community, building relational trust, and fostering relational coherence.

In this paradigm, the principal is the *culture builder*, being visible and accessible, as well as intentional about creating space for community voice and ownership. Culture-building means that we challenge the status quo, like the *paradigm of one*, the single teacher in a single classroom, or dismantle rigid subject silos in favour of more integrated, collaborative models of practice.

Equally, it calls for practical action: resourcing time for innovation, providing space for collaboration, and prioritising professional learning that nurtures agency for both teachers and students. Without these enabling conditions, even the most compelling strategy will likely remain unrealised to its full potential.

Translating vision into action

Having explored the mindset and capabilities required of leaders, we now shift from concept to practice. The following practical tools are designed to provoke reflection, conversation, and strategic clarity. Each is grounded in the understanding that leadership transformation precedes intentional cultural transformation and aligned leadership action.

These tools can stand alone or form a sequence toward a goal, depending on your context. Some offer reflective or systemic perspective (Looking Back Across Generations, Three Horizons Thinking), while others support the development of shared leadership culture and strategic coherence (The Leadership Charter, The One, The Few, The Many). Tools like Decision-Making and Action-Taking and Impact Map help move beyond insight toward purposeful, distributed action. Using these provocations with your leadership team help to ensure your vision is not just articulated but enacted boldly, collaboratively, and with intention.

Tool 1: Looking Back Across Generations

Purpose

To surface and challenge how generational experiences shape our beliefs about education. This reflection helps uncover assumptions embedded in current practices that may no longer serve today's learners.

Lens

We all bring a generational lens, shaped by our school experiences and cultural context. Mapping memories onto the four elements (learner experience, professional culture, management and systems, places, spaces, and resources) reveals how systems have evolved and highlights where they need reimagining.

Intended outcomes

- Deeper intergenerational awareness within the team
- Understanding of how past schooling influences present assumptions
- Identification of legacy practices that require transformation
- Creation of a visual artefact to support reflection and dialogue
- Stronger connection between lived experience and strategic design.

Materials

Large-format prints or display of Across the generations and When I was at school images; whiteboard or large-format paper; sticky notes; pens.

Process

Across the generations:

Reference: Adapted from McCrindle Research.

When I was at school:

1. **Personal reflection: Across the generations**
   Place yourself in a generational cohort (e.g., Gen Z, Gen X, Boomers). Recall and share a vivid memory from childhood or adolescence. Discuss changes and disruptions in your lifetime.

2. **School experience comparison: When I was at school...**
   In small groups, reflect on:
   - What was school like in your generation?
   - What is it like now?
   - Map this for each element:
     - Learner experience (How did learning feel? Who had agency?)
     - Professional culture (teacher–student dynamic)
     - Management and systems (structures and routines)
     - Places, spaces, and resources (spaces and tools used).
   - Discuss: Has the experience of school changed as much as life?

3. **Network of elements mapping**
   - On a whiteboard or sheet, draw four columns for each element.
   - Ask: What practices or assumptions from the past are still present? Which need reimagining?
   - Use sticky notes to map insights.

4. **Reflection and display**
   - Step back to review the whole map
   - Identify emerging patterns and hidden assumptions
   - Keep the map visible to allow for ongoing contributions.

Tool 2: The Leadership Charter

Purpose
To co-create a leadership team agreement that reflects shared values, fosters trust, and strengthens collaboration.

Lens
Clarity and connection behind the scenes are essential before stepping onto the *front stage* of leadership. This process cultivates intentional and aligned values/culture among leaders.

Intended outcomes
- Shared agreement on leadership values and expectations
- Increased relational trust and safety
- A co-developed artefact to guide team behaviour
- Ongoing rituals to maintain alignment and reflection.

Materials
Sticky notes; whiteboard or large chart paper; pens.

Credit: Adapted from a process used by Dr Stephen Harris.

Process
For groups of 6–12 people, such as boards, close-working teams.

1. **Build social capital – What do we each bring?**
    - Arrange chairs in a circle or around a table. Each person writes their own name on a sticky note and places it at their place/on their seat.
    - Everyone stands with a sticky note pad and a pen in hand, stepping away from their place.
    - Write a positive, encouraging strength for each team member and leave it at their place.
    - Each person returns to their place and reflects on what they received.

2. **Define shared values – How might we work?**
    - Return to your place.
    - Each person writes three values that matter for working well together – put them together on the table or on a whiteboard.
    - Group and synthesise into three to five core shared values.

3. **Needs-based dialogue – Bringing our best**
   - Each participant answers on a sticky note: What do I need from the team to be my best self?
   - Share, discuss, and document common and unique needs.

4. **Draft the charter – Review**
   - Co-write a team statement/charter summarising how the group commits to working together.

5. **Commitment – How I will grow**
   - Each person names one leadership behaviour or value they will intentionally grow.

6. **Feedback and rituals**
   - Agree on a check-in rhythm (e.g., monthly or termly) to revisit and reflect on the charter.
   - Invite new team members to review and contribute when joining.

Tool 3: The One, The Few, The Many

Purpose

To build sustainable, human-centred leadership by helping individuals connect their inner self (The One), strengthen trust within the team (The Few), and extend collective influence (The Many).

Lens

Strategic change starts from within. Amid urgency and task-focus, leadership teams risk losing the self-awareness, trust, and alignment essential for clarity and coherence. The One, The Few, The Many foregrounds the human side of change by acknowledging internal resistance, emphasising *backstage* trust-building, and reinforcing the need for intentional alignment before stepping onto the *front stage*. This session supports teams to align, unite behind shared purpose, and lead with clarity.

Intended outcomes

- Increased self-awareness of leadership styles and triggers
- Stronger team trust through story-sharing and aligned values
- Greater cohesion and relational safety
- Clear alignment from internal purpose to external influence.

Materials

Print diagram or display of The One, The Few, The Many; sticky notes, pens.

Process

Gather your core team.

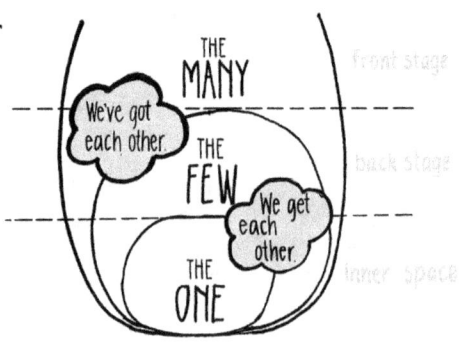

Part 1: The One – Inner space

Individual reflection:
- What has shaped my leadership story?
- What narratives or patterns emerge when facing uncertainty?
- Share with The Few.
- Optional tool (e.g., Gallup Strengths or values self-assessment)

Part 2: The Few – Back stage
- We get each other: In small groups, share leadership reflections.

Discuss: What do we need from each other to feel safe and confident?
- We've got each other: How do we reach a working consensus? While we may not all necessarily agree, can we reach a united position as we face *The Many*?

Part 3: The Many – Front stage
- Map who The Many are in your world; a bubble or spider diagram works well (staff, students, parents, broader community).
- Scenario: How do we show up together on the front stage during a key initiative?
- Debrief: What shifts in team behaviour would improve our collective impact?

Closing
- Each person names one practice they commit to strengthening.
- Optional: Display your shared team statement in a communal space.
- Clarify immediate next steps for building cohesion and influence.
- Develop an accountability schedule.

Tool 4: Decision-Making and Action-Taking

Purpose

When faced with competing demands on multiple fronts, to analyse the nature of challenges and apply the appropriate strategy for action based on the Cynefin Framework.

Lens

Not all problems are equal. Some require process; others demand innovation or rapid triage. Matching response to context is key. This Cynefin Framework is applied to identify the characteristics of different challenges and adapt decision-making strategies. Complex challenges often require the application of a design process, where the team works with confidence and optimism to a seek a way forward.

Intended outcomes

- Map the scope of challenges/problems
- Distinguish between simple, complicated, complex, and chaotic problems (see the Explainer below)
- Choose fitting approaches for each challenge
- Align resources and actions strategically.

Materials

Decision-Making and Action-Taking diagram (drawn or printed in large format); sticky notes; markers.

Credit: Snowden & Boone (2007); McCandless & Lipmanowicz (2013).

Process

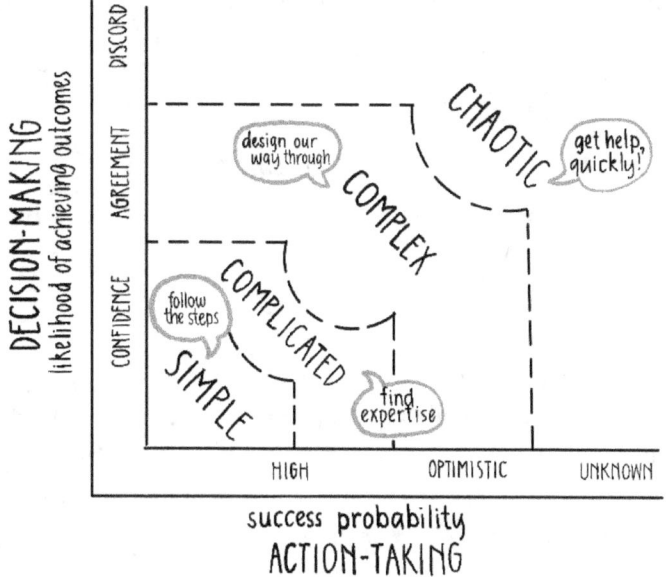

Gather your team. See the Explainer below for the outline of each problem type.

1. Identify all current challenges, one per sticky note.
2. Plot challenges on the matrix: Simple, Complicated, Complex, Chaotic.
3. Identify which need expertise, design, or urgent triage.
4. Create action plans based on type.
5. Group reflection: Step back and observe patterns. Ask:
   - Where do we need to focus our collective time?
   - Where do most of our challenges sit?
   - What might this tell us about our strategy and prioritising?

Action planning based on type:
- For **Simple and Complicated** problems: Assign actions, timelines, and responsibilities. Find expertise.
- For **Complex** problems: Apply a design process for exploration, inquiry, or prototyping. Allocate project time and responsibilities.
- For **Chaotic** items: Triage immediately; decide who needs to be involved, and what is the first stabilising step.

Explainer

Simple = *high agreement + high confidence*
- Follow known procedures or checklists
- Low complexity, clear steps

> If we stick with the plan, we'll get a good result

Complicated = *high confidence + need for expertise*
- Make a plan and get an expert
- Outcomes are knowable

> There is a way to fix this, but we don't have the expertise

Complex = *agreement + optimism*
- Progress through iteration and co-design
- Outcomes emerge through learning and adaptation

> We have optimism that we can find a way through, but the path isn't clear

Chaotic = *unknowns + discord or urgency*
- Immediate intervention; stabilise before planning
- First, act to restore order

> Help! We don't know what to do, where to start

Tool 5: Three Horizons Thinking

Purpose

Applying strategic foresight through applying Three Horizons Thinking to equip teams with a structured method for exploring current assumptions, envisioning desired futures, and identifying actionable steps to move from the present to the possible. This tool helps teams manage uncertainty and plan with intentionality in a time of transformation.

Lens

The Three Horizons Framework was developed by Bill Sharpe (2013), a futures thinker, researcher, and innovator. His work has helped leaders to think beyond short-term fixes toward sustainable, systemic transformation.

- **Horizon 1** represents today's dominant practices and assumptions.
- **Horizon 2** is the entrepreneurial and adaptive space in between – the site of innovation, tension, and transition.
- **Horizon 3** reflects the visionary future we aspire to.

This framework enables leaders to examine continuity, disruption, and transformation simultaneously.

Intended outcomes

- Increased strategic awareness of current realities versus emerging possibilities
- Shared language for thinking across short-, mid-, and long-term horizons
- A visual map of where innovation is needed and where existing practices dominate
- Identification of concrete next steps
- A stronger culture of adaptive leadership and future-focused planning.

Materials

Large-format printed or drawn version (A1/butcher's paper/newsprint) of the Three Horizons Framework diagram; pens; sticky notes.

Credit: Sharpe (2013); https://www.h3uni.org/facilitation-guide/three-horizon-mapping-guide/; Goodwin (2020).

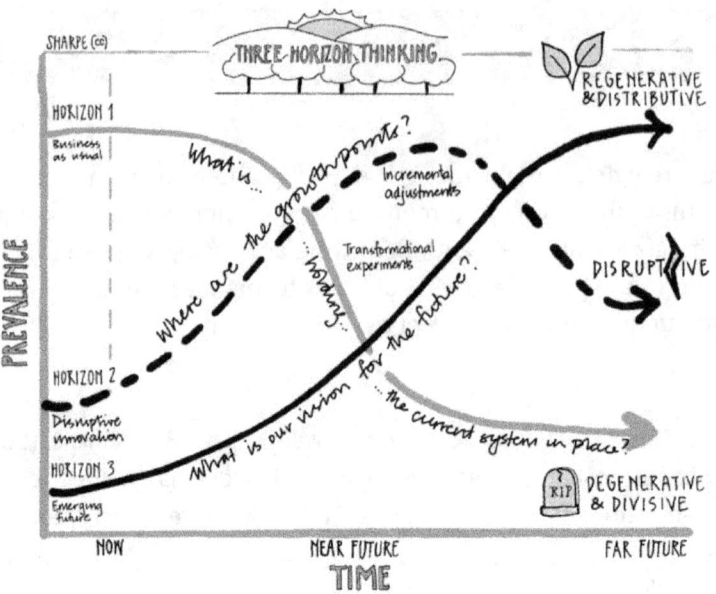
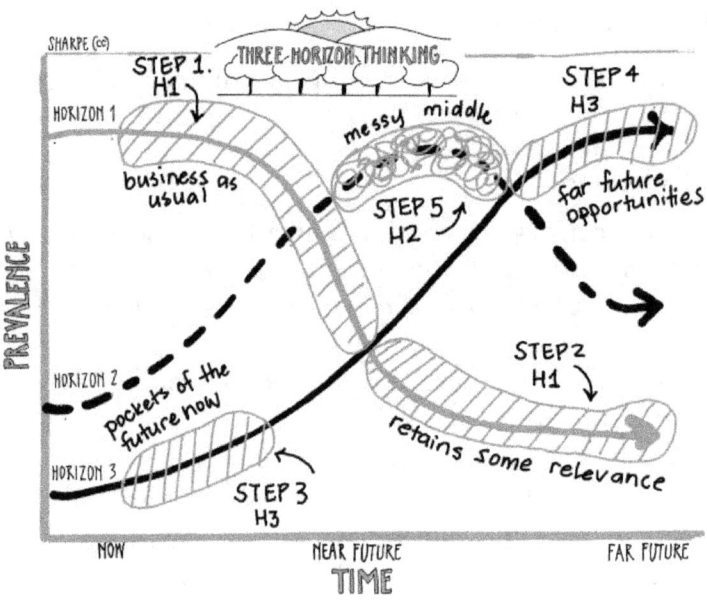

Process

1. **STEP 1/H1** Business as usual – no longer fit for purpose?
   - What evidence do you see around you that suggests the current system is under strain?
   - What shows a decreasing fit with emerging conditions?
   - What is currently failing?

2. **STEP 2 /H1** Current practice – remains fit for purpose?
   - Are there current practices that might remain in the *near future* or *far future*?

3. **STEP 3 /H3** Near future – causing ripples
   - What is an emergent trend?
   - What are the pockets of the future that you see?
   - What are the sources of those disruptions?

4. **STEP 4 /H3** Far future opportunities – visionary insight
   - What do we see is made possible in the future?
   - What parts of our vision/mission/values show alignment with these opportunities?
   - What long-term trends are taking us toward these changes?

5. **STEP 5/H2** Emergent future – what's in the messy middle?
   - What is being disrupted?
   - What innovations do we know about that might be growth points for future systems?
   - How are people navigating this?

Close the session with a focused discussion:
- Which current assumptions are most at risk of becoming obsolete?
- Which changes are both promising and ready to be actioned now?
- Which innovations hold the greatest potential to make progress?

This debrief grounds the foresight process in strategic clarity, surfacing where to focus energy next and how to build a pathway from the present to a preferred future.

Tool 6: Impact Map

Purpose

To evaluate the ripple effects of recent or planned initiatives on people, their workload, wellbeing, and professional culture. This activity helps to surface potential impacts of decisions or projects, to identify what's making a positive difference and prioritise energy and resources accordingly.

Lens

All change has consequences. Impact Map invites you to pause, reflect, and assess how decisions or projects are/might be experienced by staff. It shifts the conversation from *What are we going to do?* to an empathic stance: *What is the impact?* By visualising and evaluating these effects, we can make informed decisions about what to amplify, what to adjust, and what we may need to let go.

Intended outcomes

- A visual map of current and recent initiatives, including their real and perceived impact on staff
- Shared understanding of pressure points, overlaps, and initiatives that are creating value
- Identification of two to three priorities for focus, investment, or scaling
- Pre-empt potential culture-builder and culture-breaker impacts
- Commitment to actions that amplify what's working and dampen what's causing friction or fatigue.

Materials

Whiteboard or large-format sheets (A1/butcher's paper/newsprint); sticky notes; markers; pens.

Credit: Adapted from the suite of tools in PEP Worldwide (2019).

Process

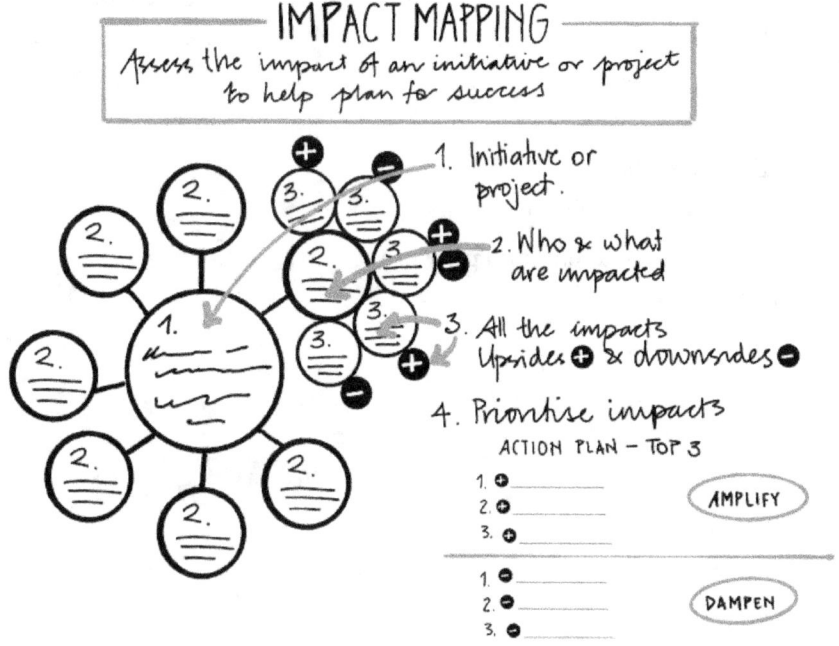

Gather your leadership team.

1. **Context: An initiative/project you will be working on.**

   Draw a circle in the centre of the sheet of paper.

   Write one new initiative/project in the centre.

2. **Who and what will be directly impacted by this initiative/project?**

   Create a spider diagram with each *who* and *what* radiating from the centre circle.

   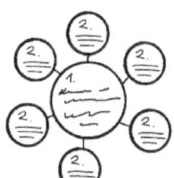

3. **Identify impacts.**

   For each *who* and *what*, list all the impacts. Think about the upsides and the downsides.

4. **Prioritise impacts.**

   Assess each impact and determine the top three for each.

   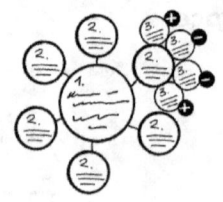

5. **Action planning.**

   How can we amplify what's working?

   What can we do to dampen pressure or harm?

The Elements Unpacked

Once the leadership foundation is laid and is anchored in trust, clarity, and shared purpose, the next step is to turn outward and explore the four interconnected elements in greater detail. You'll find an explanation of their purpose and function within this model, followed by practical activities to assess, activate, and evolve your context. Together, these shape the learning environment in your school.

The elements form the conceptual framework for strategic design. They are not isolated elements, but a network of interdependent elements that evolve in harmony to create meaningful, sustainable change. They can help us move beyond abstract aspirations into the lived reality of school life.

As with all elements of this field guide, you are invited to start where the energy and interest might be, whether this involves improving learner agency, strengthening staff culture, untangling legacy systems, or reimagining physical learning environments. The path is not linear, but the framework exists as a scaffold to guide you.

Chapter 8
Learner Experience: Why We Exist

The focus on *learner experience* represents the overarching vision for the school. A community vision begins with the learners/students and can help to identify opportunities for transformation and explore practical strategies for fostering deeper learning, engagement, agency, and future readiness.

The learner experience element assesses and redefines student life in your school:

- What does our aspiration for learning look like?
- How is our vision outworked in the everyday experiences of learners?
- What structures, pedagogies, and models enable greater student agency?

Why this matters

The overarching purpose is to support the shift from a legacy model of school that leaves little room for student agency. The world students are entering is fundamentally different from the one experienced by previous generations. Success today requires a fresh set of evolving skills, which include adaptability, creativity, problem-solving, and agency. These qualities thrive in transforming learning environments.

Drawing on the work of Jenny Anderson and Dr Rebecca Winthrop in *The Disengaged Teen: Helping Kids to Learn Better, Feel Better and Live Better*, the learner experience can be influenced by four engagement modes that students might shift between:

- **Resister:** Ignores or opposes undertaking tasks, skips class, finds excuses, or acts out, voicing their reasons why something is not working for them.
- **Passenger:** Coasts along, consistently doing the bare minimum and complaining that school is pointless.

- **Achiever:** Shows up, does the work, and consistently achieves high grades. Their self-worth can become tied to high performance. Their disengagement is invisible, fuelled by a fear of failure, putting them at risk of mental health challenges.
- **Explorer:** Driven by internal curiosity rather than just external expectations, they investigate the questions they care about and persist to achieve goals.

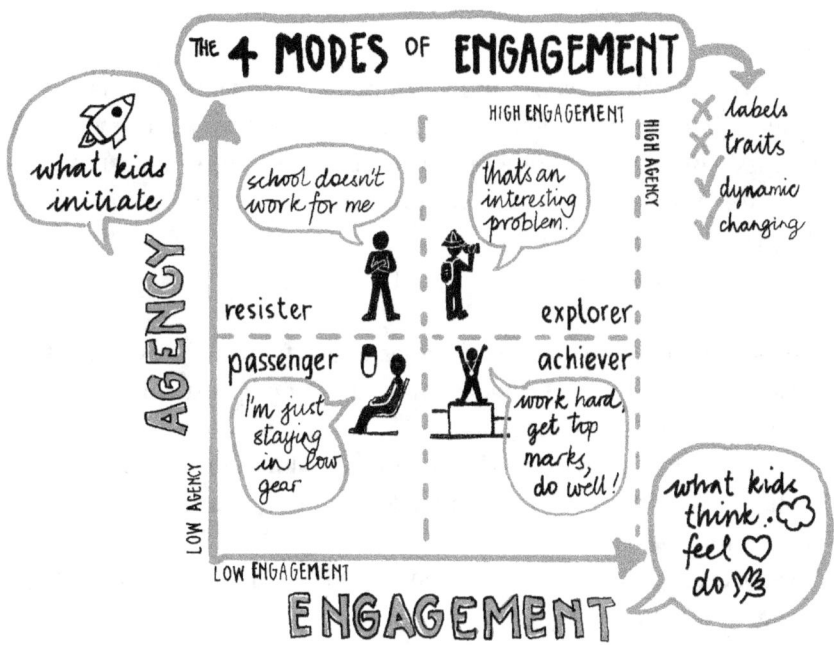

These categories capture distinct ways students engage with learning. Traditionally, society has valued the *achiever* mode as the goal. However, it's the *explorer* mode that equips learners for the future. By mapping these perspectives, we can gain deeper insights into the varied experiences of students, helping to design more inclusive and responsive learning environments.

Practical tools for learner experience help us to design the school experience from an empathic perspective. The Empathy Map and Journey Map are helpful touchpoints whenever decisions are being made that will impact the learners. Pulse Check: Learner Experience begins to grow a shared understanding of the current situation and future possibilities.

Tool 7: Empathy Map

Purpose

To engage in deep dialogue that uncovers the lived experience of students by developing learner personas. This activity supports teams to think beyond assumptions and step into the world of their learners, capturing both challenges and opportunities to inform the design of the school experience.

Lens

A transforming school sees students not as passive recipients, but as individuals navigating complex emotional, cognitive, and relational landscapes. This activity applies a user-experience mindset to explore how students *see, hear, feel, think, and do* within the school day, centred on both challenges and opportunities.

Intended outcomes

- Develop learner personas as reference points for future design work
- Heighten empathy for diverse learner experiences, particularly those who are disengaged or unseen
- Increase alignment between leadership decisions and learner realities
- A shift in perspective from planning *for* students to designing *with* a deep understanding
- A set of artefacts that can be referenced in future planning, leadership discussions, or co-design work
- Develop foundational thinking for designing agency-rich, inclusive learning environments with a user focus.

Materials

Large-format Empathy Map (printed or drawn on A1/butcher's paper/newsprint); sticky notes and markers; visual quadrant with axes: **Agency** (low to high) and **Engagement** (low to high); Empathy Map with figure.

Credit: Anderson and Winthrop (2025).

Process

Work in groups of three to five.

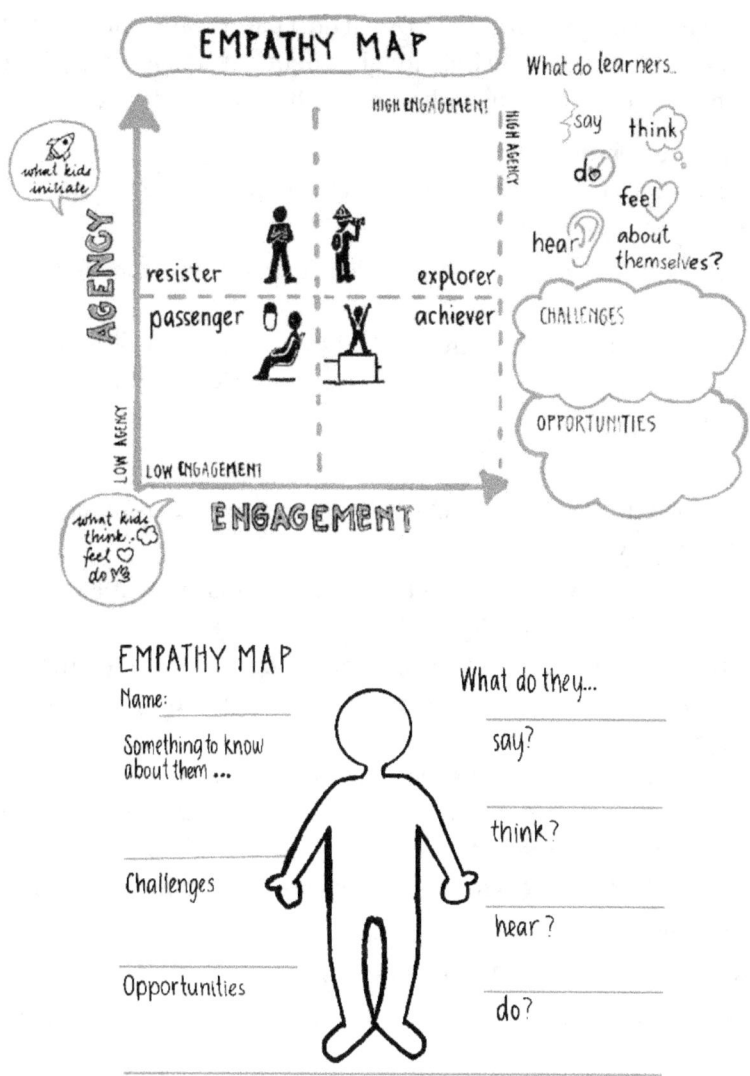

1. **Agree on a persona to explore**

   You could use the four learner modes from *The Disengaged Teen*:
   - **Resister** – overt disengagement, including defiance
   - **Passenger** – compliant but uninvested, doing the bare minimum
   - **Achiever** – identifies as successful in conventional terms; consistently meets or exceeds academic expectations
   - **Explorer** – intrinsically motivated learner driven by curiosity; seeks knowledge, asks questions, initiates learning.

Learner Experience: Why We Exist

Or develop your own personas based on a particular need. An Empathy Map does not identify an individual student but creates aggregated representations of learners who display the particular behaviours.

2. **Shape the persona**
   Working in groups of three to five, each group adopts one persona. Choose between two methods:
   - **Short form**: Draw on your experience and shared knowledge of students.
   - **Longer form**: Gather anonymised student insight to craft more representative personas (e.g., through observations, interviews or focus groups).

3. **Complete the Empathy Map**
   Using the Empathy Map template, explore each dimension of the learner's experience:
   - **Something to know about them: Who is your persona?** Give them a name and personality/backstory.
   - **What do they say?** How do they talk about school or learning?
   - **What do they think?** What internal beliefs, worries, or hopes do they hold?
   - **What do they feel?** What emotions dominate their day?
   - **What do they hear?** What messages are they receiving from peers, teachers, and parents?
   - **What do they do?** What behaviours are observable in class or around school?

   End with two reflection prompts:
   - **Challenges** – Where do they experience friction, confusion, or disconnection?
   - **Opportunities** – Where could agency and engagement be strengthened?

4. **Gallery walk and dialogue**
   Display each group's Empathy Map. Facilitate a reflective walk and discussion:
   - What common patterns or contrasts are emerging across personas?
   - Which personas feel most prevalent or under-represented in our context?
   - How do current teaching and learning practices support or hinder each learner?

5. **Debrief and apply**

    Use the following prompts to conclude:
    - Which insights most challenge our assumptions?
    - How might these personas shape our planning, pedagogy, or systems?

    Identify three to five high-leverage areas for improvement, and link them back to the four domains:
    - Learner experience
    - Professional culture
    - Management and systems
    - Places, spaces, and resources.

Tool 8: Journey Map

Purpose

To reflect on the current student experience and identify inconsistencies between the aspirational vision and the lived reality of school life. This mapping process helps teams surface opportunities for improvement, celebrate what's working, and align practices more intentionally with their strategic vision.

Lens

A transforming school is built around the learner experience. This activity invites us to view the school day through the eyes of a student, developing empathy and recognising how daily routines either support or undermine the intended learning culture. It's a step toward designing with clarity, care, and coherence.

Intended outcomes

- A **big-picture perspective** on the learner experience that highlights both alignment and gaps
- Greater **empathy and insight** into how students engage with daily routines and structures
- **Clarity on actionable priorities** for improving the learner journey
- A tangible artefact that can be referenced in future planning, leadership discussions, or co-design work
- Momentum for more **agile, learner-centred design decisions** that build from real experience rather than assumption.

Materials

Large-format sheets (A1/butcher's paper/newsprint); sticky notes; markers.

Process

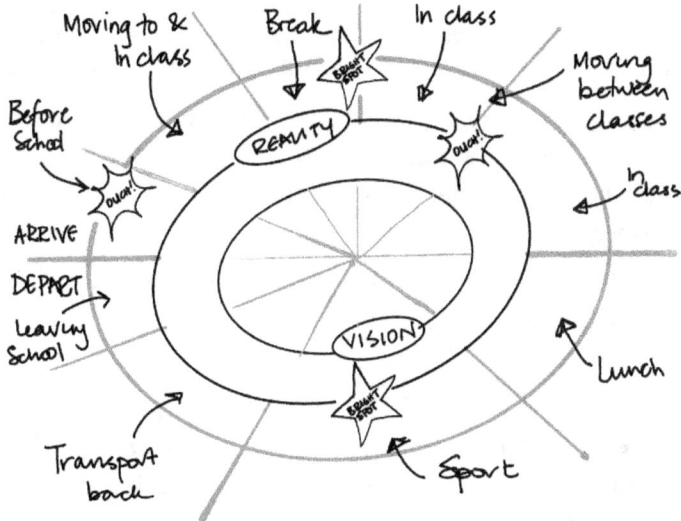

1. **Work in small groups** (three to four people). Choose either:
   - A specific **student persona** (see Empathy Map persona)
   - A **cohort with a shared experience** (e.g., Year 9 students, disengaged boys, new to the school).

   Decide on the mapping scope: *a typical school day*, or a representative week.

2. **Map the scope – *Reality versus Vision*.** Use a timeline or concentric circle format to create two parallel tracks:
   - **Reality track** – What learners currently experience at each key moment
   - **Vision track** – What the ideal experience could look and feel like.

   Key time points across the day may include:
   - Arrival
   - Learning sessions
   - Breaks
   - Transitions
   - Specialist sessions
   - Lunchtime
   - Departure.

If time permits, gather real-time data through shadowing, student interviews, or observational notes.

3. **Identify key touchpoints** – For each time point across a day, use sticky notes to document:
   - **Bright spots** – moments of connection, joy, or successful alignment with your school vision
   - **Pain points** – moments of disconnection, stress, or structural obstacles.

   Use colour-coded markers or dots to highlight:
   - Areas of strong alignment
   - Areas of tension or inconsistency
   - Emerging opportunities.

4. **Enrich with student insight** – Add student quotes, observed behaviours, or anecdotes to humanise the map. This grounds abstract design conversations in lived experience.

5. **Discussion**
   - What patterns are emerging across the learner journey?
   - Where do we observe the biggest gaps between vision and reality?
   - What's already working that we should amplify?
   - Where might small shifts yield significant gains?
   - What needs to be fundamentally reimagined?

6. **Prioritise for action**

   Identify three to five high-leverage areas for improvement, and link them back to the four domains:
   - Learner experience
   - Professional culture
   - Management and systems
   - Places, spaces, and resources.

   Encourage each team to define one or two **next steps** that can be trialled immediately.

Tool 9: Pulse Check: Learner Experience

Purpose

To evaluate and improve the current experience of learners by surfacing what's working well, and where improvements are needed. This tool provides a structured, empathic approach to examine the school experience through the lens of student equity, engagement, and agency.

Lens

A future-focused school intentionally monitors the learner experience to remain responsive, relevant, and inclusive. This tool brings a critical eye to the present by asking: *Are we living our vision?* It invites a cycle of continuous improvement that values both affirmation and honest critique.

Intended outcomes

- Stronger alignment between current practice and the school's aspirational learner vision
- Prioritised actions to address areas that may be lacking
- A shared visual artefact that can spark strategic conversations and planning
- A foundation for ongoing learner-centred improvement cycles.

Materials

Printed or drawn Learner Experience: What's Working Well? and Even Better if..., as shown below, on large-format sheets (A2 or A3/butcher's paper/newsprint); markers; pens; sticky notes.

Process

1. **Frame the activity** – Introduce the goal of the session: to evaluate how current learner experience aligns with the school's vision/aspiration. You may choose to focus on a specific year level, subject, or learner group.

2. **Affirm: What's working well**? Invite participants to reflect on and document current practices or moments in the learner journey that support your school's desired learning culture.

    Prompt examples:
    - Where are students showing genuine engagement or agency?
    - What have we noticed?
    - What systems or routines are positively supporting learning?

3. **Challenge: Even better if**… Now turn to areas for growth. Encourage participants to name what is misaligned, missing, or could be strengthened to better serve students.

    Prompt examples:
    - What feels outdated, confusing, or unmotivating for learners?
    - What have we noticed?
    - Where are students disengaging – and why?
    - What are potential opportunities for improvement?

4. **Thematic synthesis** – As a team, group sticky notes into themes. Use subheadings or categories (e.g., classroom culture, assessment, transitions, student voice) to clarify key areas of focus.

    Look for:
    - Repetition or resonance across responses
    - Differences between staff perspectives and student insights
    - Personas that are under-supported or over-represented.

5. **Prioritise and plan** – Identify two to three high-impact opportunities for immediate or short-term action. For each, consider:
    - What small shift could we implement now?
    - Who will lead the next step or prototype a solution?
    - How will we follow up or evaluate change?

Chapter 9
Professional Culture: How We Work

A transforming school culture doesn't happen by chance. It is cultivated with intention, where collaboration replaces isolation, and professional learning becomes embedded in the flow of daily work. This domain builds the human heart of the school, the relational landscape where trust is built, purpose is shared, and growth becomes collective.

In this section, we explore how to design and sustain a professional culture that aligns with your vision, strengthens staff agency, and builds the coherence needed to transform learner experience.

Why this matters

When we speak about school culture, our intention is focused on transforming the learner experience. But that transformation is only possible when the adults, the entire staff, take responsibility for cultivating the desired professional culture that underpins the vision and is an expression of the values.

From my research I concluded that the leaders are the culture-builders, the staff are the culture-bearers, and the culture represents the milieu of students. It may be encouraging and vibrant, or controlling and stifling. The attractiveness or otherwise of the prevailing culture is not the responsibility of the students, but how the adults represent it.

A hierarchical, compliance-driven environment leaves little space for the voice and agency of the staff. In contrast, a thriving workplace culture fosters a sense of purpose and empowerment. People feel valued and united by a shared mission and energised by a compelling vision for the future. Building a strong and positive professional culture fosters psychological safety, shared ownership, and adaptive mindsets.

It is founded on trust and cultivated through a vision that is not just known, but collectively owned and brought to life through behaviours, rituals and routines, and structures that reflect the espoused values. To reach this requires the courage to challenge longstanding assumptions, to assess the relevance of traditions, and to rethink organisational models. While not everything is ruled out, there should be an understanding that not everything will necessarily remain, either.

You are encouraged to reflect deeply on your current workplace culture, explore practical strategies for building trust and connection, and consider how to create the conditions where both teachers and students can truly thrive through a co-created *team agreement*.

The tools outlined in *learner experience* provide an important foundation for the professional culture, as they highlight the 'why'. From a culture perspective, the tools and activities explored around *professional culture* provide the critical foundation to support the future-oriented vision and purpose. The Empathy Map and Journey Map activities in the previous section can provide a reference to guide the articulation of the desired culture.

With a focus on the back stage, Agentic Learning Design is situated within the professional culture domain because it represents a fundamental shift in how educators reframe their role, beyond curriculum planning and content delivery, becoming designers of engaging learning. This transformation reshapes professional identity and practice, requiring teachers to work together around a shared purpose. By focusing on how teachers holistically design learning experiences, a culture of co-design emerges. It is through this collaborative design culture that schools can create consistent, enabling conditions for learner agency to flourish.

Finally, the complementary activity of this section, Pulse Check: Professional Culture, evaluates the current situation and highlights future possibilities.

Tool 10: Team Agreement

Purpose

To intentionally build a foundation for team culture by co-creating a shared agreement that outlines values, expectations, and working norms.

Lens

Physical proximity alone does not build collaborative culture. Purposeful rituals, routines, and agreed norms create a sense of safety and ownership essential for shared teaching environments.

Intended outcomes

- A co-created team agreement defining shared purpose, values, and ways of working
- Greater empathy and understanding among team members
- Reduced assumptions and future conflict
- Establishment of relational rituals and routines that support sustainable collaboration.

Materials

Large paper (A1 or butcher's paper); sticky notes; markers; pens.

Credit: Adapted from a process used by colleagues at SCIL 2012-16.

Process

Groups from four to six are ideal. With larger groups, work in sub-teams then join for synthesis.

1. **Setting the stage**
   - Share the why: We are building our professional culture by design, not by default.
   - Emphasise that this is a living agreement to revisit and evolve.

2. **Team connection**

   Each person shares either:
   - This is something you don't know about me, or
   - A defining moment that made me who I am today.

   (2 minutes per person; time-keeper appointed)

3. **Shared purpose statement**
   - Use 1-2-4-All: reflect, pair, share.
   - Prompt: Why is collaboration important to me? What do I hope we achieve?
   - Synthesise into a one-sentence team purpose: *Our team exists to... so that...*

4. **'If this is you...' spider map**

   Create a bubble diagram. Write in the centre: *If this is you...* Then add the other bubbles around it:
   - I'm passionate about...
   - The best way to communicate with me on an issue is...
   - My treat from the café is...
   - To start my day well I need...
   - An area I'm keen to grow in this year is...
   - Something I want you to know about me...
   - I can get frustrated when...

   Each team member responds to the prompts on sticky notes (as shown below).

5. **Defining agreements**

   Identify five to seven team norms that frame a working consensus – e.g., *We agree to assume positive intent* or *We agree to raise concerns early.*

6. **Commitment and rituals**
   - Review and affirm the agreement together.
   - Decide how frequently it will be revisited (e.g., monthly check-in)
   - Share it with each new team member and invite their contribution.

Tool 11: Agentic Learning Design

Purpose

To scaffold the *professional culture* (how we work) from a focus on delivering content to becoming designers of learning. This supports the design of learning experiences that support teacher-led, teacher-supported, and student-initiated learning. This process ensures that the design of learning includes the enabling constraints, such as curriculum requirements and school culture norms.

Lens

True agency is not about simply offering choices; it requires intentional design, developing opportunities for agentic learning experiences with a careful balance of structure and freedom, guidance, and autonomy to initiate learning. This process frames teachers as designers where students can gradually assume greater responsibility, making choices that are meaningful, challenging, and connected to real-world purposes.

Intended outcomes

- A shared understanding of agentic learning
- A co-created design framework that balances curriculum outcomes with student-driven inquiry
- Practical strategies for building scaffolds and structures that support increasing learner autonomy
- Identification of the spatial and organisational enablers needed to foster agency
- Greater confidence among educators to shift from traditional delivery models to coaching and facilitation roles.

Materials

Agentic Learning Design printed on large-format sheets (A1/butcher's paper/newsprint); sticky notes; pens; markers.

Process

Gather your co-design team. Display Agentic Learning Design in the *war room* to build over time.

AGENTIC LEARNING DESIGN

See annotated Agentic Learning Design below.

1. **Curriculum/disciplines** – Identify curriculum areas, capabilities, and broader skills that will be embedded through agentic approaches.
2. **Learner aspirations** – Co-create a future-facing design question – for example:

    How might we create the learning environment to support deeper learning and nurture agency and engagement?
3. **Who's in?** – Gather your design team.
4. **Spatial implications** – Along the way, consider how spaces will be organised to support student agency:
    - Layouts
    - Visible planning spaces
    - Zones for collaboration, quiet reflection, making, and presenting.

    Think about inside and outside, on-site, and off-site opportunities.

Mapping the journey – beginning with the end in mind

5. **Big idea and guiding question** – Defining the central theme or problem that will anchor the learning experience. This helps the team align on the overarching purpose of the design.
6. **Mountain top** – Define the tangible outcome that students will produce/work towards, such as projects, products, exhibitions, innovation.
7. **Celebration** – Identify ways to elevate and celebrate agentic learning. Could students present at a conference, showcase at an exhibition, or pitch ideas to authentic audiences?

Checkpoints

8. **Empathy mapping:** Step into the learner's shoes. What does a day look like when they have agency? What supports do they need?
9. **Enabling constraints:** Identify necessary boundaries, e.g., curriculum requirements, school-based learner frameworks, resourcing.
10. **How will we know? (Part 1):** Define success criteria for agency (e.g., initiative-taking, decision-making, collaboration) and how progress will be assessed.
11. **How will we know? (Part 2)** Use iterative check-ins with students to evaluate how agentic practices are developing and adjust scaffolding accordingly. Build student voice into the evaluation process itself.

Getting creative

12. **Entry event** – Design an opening challenge, provocation, or real-world hook that immediately hands some decision-making or ownership over to the learners.

Engaged learning criteria

13. **Learning why** – Clearly articulate to students the *why* behind agentic learning. Why does this matter for them, now and into the future?
14. **Learning what** – Identify the essential knowledge and skills learners need, but leave room for inquiry, passion, and direction.
15. **Learning how** – Plan scaffolds, tools, and coaching strategies that support students in taking increasing ownership over their learning pathways.

Practicalities – getting it done

16. **Roles and responsibilities** – Clarify how teachers will work as *coaches, guides, and facilitators* rather than deliverers of content.
17. **Resources** – Identify tools, tech, spaces, and mindsets needed to support student-driven learning.
18. **Anything else?** – Include time allocations, feedback loops, and documentation tools to track student decision-making and growth.

Documenting: As a guide, the shared tool can be documented as shown below. Adapt terminology to suit your own context.

AGENTIC LEARNING DESIGN FRAMEWORK				
Grade/Year Level:				
Who's in?				
Big Idea				
Curriculum/Discipline				
Guiding question				
Learner aspirations				
Entry event				
Mountain top				
Celebration				
Engaged Learning	Learning How			
	Learning Why			
	Learning What:	Must encounter:		Might encounter:
		Encourage interests and passions:		Learn skills:
Practicalities	Roles and responsibilities:	Resources:		Anything else:
Checkpoints				
Enabling constraints	Time			
	Resourcing			
	Curriculum, culture and compliance requirements	Internal:		
		External:		
Empathy mapping	Student persona	1		
		2		
		3		
		4		
Spatial implications	Inside:		Outside:	
	Offsite:		Onsite	

Tool 12: Pulse Check: Professional Culture

Purpose

To evaluate how your current team culture supports trust, growth, and collaboration.

To evaluate and improve the professional culture by surfacing what's working well, and where improvements or refinements are needed. This tool provides a structured, empathic approach to examine the professional culture through shared values, decision-making, and practices.

Lens

A transforming school intentionally monitors its professional culture to create an aligned workplace that lives and breathes its values. This tool brings a critical eye to the present by asking: *Are we living our values?* It invites a cycle of continuous improvement that values both affirmation and honest critique.

Intended outcomes

- Recognise strengths in professional relationships and shared vision
- Identify cultural friction points (e.g., silos, misalignment with values)
- Plan culture-building strategies rooted in dialogue, respect, and growth
- A shared visual artefact that can spark strategic conversations and planning.

Materials

Printed or drawn Professional Culture: What's Working Well? and Even Better if..., as shown below, on large-format sheets (A2 or A3/butcher's paper/newsprint); markers; pens; sticky notes.

Process

> Professional Culture
>
> What's working well?
>
> Even better if...

1. **Frame the activity** – Introduce the goal of the session: to evaluate how current professional culture aligns with the school's values and supports the desired learner experience.

   The activity is best when undertaken in groups of four to five, with responses then aggregated.

2. **Affirm: What's working well?** Affirm aspects of professional culture that support the vision for learner experience.

   Prompt examples:
   - Where can you see alignment with values and the vision to support learner experience?
   - What systems or routines are positively impacting the desired professional culture?

3. **Challenge: Even better if...** Now turn to areas for growth. Encourage participants to name what is misaligned, missing, or could be strengthened to better serve an aligned culture.

   Prompt examples:
   - What feels outdated, confusing, or unmotivating for staff?
   - Where is the culture and practice unaligned with the vision?
   - What are potential opportunities for improvement?

4. **Thematic synthesis** – As a team, group sticky notes into themes. Use subheadings or categories (e.g., classroom culture, assessment, transitions, student voice) to clarify key areas of focus.

5. **Prioritise and plan** – Identify two or three **high-impact opportunities** for immediate or short-term action. For each, consider:
    - What small shift could we implement now?
    - Who will lead the next step or prototype a solution?
    - How will we follow up or evaluate change?

Chapter 10
Management and Systems: How We Organise

Learner experience and *professional culture* are grounded in human connection represented by relationships, trust, belonging, and shared purpose. These elements don't thrive in isolation; they are enabled by the systems, structures, and processes that sit beneath them. This is where management (as a process, not role) becomes more than logistics; it is the engine that supports people to do their best work. When systems and structures are intentionally designed to reflect the school's values, they empower: timetables can support deeper learning, clarity of process reduces friction, and resource flows reflect priorities. In this way, *management and systems* become empowering rather than restricting, supporting people by design, not just by intention.

Why this matters

Many schools and organisations operate within legacy systems built for efficiency and control. These systems are not necessarily developed with the agility required for innovation and prioritising opportunities for human connection. Often these ways of working remain unopposed because 'isn't this what schools always do?'

The shift from rigid, top-down processes to dynamic ones, enabling a culture that can support agency, growth, and collaboration, occurs through intentionally designing systems that align with a vision for learning. However, without adopting a design mindset, even the most forward-thinking school vision can be limited by ill-fitting operational structures.

To ensure that systems serve purpose, rather than tradition for its own sake, you are encouraged to examine existing operational structures to understand how they enable or restrict the potential for a transforming school. This section invites you and your team to critically assess your school's systems, explore strategies for organisational transformation, and apply practical tools to align structures with purpose.

To transform schools beyond the limitations of legacy systems, we need a new kind of thinking, one that sees the school as a living ecosystem which needs to thrive rather than a machine that is 'well-oiled'. The Regenerative Ecocycle facilitates this mindset. It goes beyond sustaining the status quo and instead seeks to restore, revitalise, and create the conditions for long-term flourishing. Rather than controlling change from the top down, applying regenerative thinking cultivates growth, shining a light on culture, capability, and capacity. The goal is to disrupt habitual patterns that no longer serve, and intentionally design structures that reflect deep purpose and interconnectedness. This is especially critical when addressing entrenched management systems that maintain routines, roles, and reporting lines that may seem efficient, but can dampen fresh ideas, autonomy, and human connection.

Legacy systems tend to default toward control, yet regenerative leaders move the organisation into a more dynamic state, one where experimentation is encouraged, energy and resources flows toward what matters, and outdated structures are consciously let go. This is where the Regenerative Ecocycle becomes a powerful tool. Borrowed from ecology, the ecocycle reframes leadership decision-making around four natural phases: *birth*, *maturity*, *creative destruction*, and *renewal*.

This lens is applied to map how time, resources, and attention are distributed across initiatives and systems. Along the way, we identify what should be maintained, what is thriving, and what needs to be reimagined/renewed (or discarded). Instead of reacting to change or pushing reform through outdated processes, the Regenerative Ecocycle invites a pattern of intentional disruption and renewal, fostering resilience and adaptability across the whole school ecosystem.

For example, the Regenerative Ecocycle might highlight the rigidity of the timetable. By working through the process, we can address the subject silos through the ensuing shared dialogue. Breaking Down Silos provides a way to address the subject silos through focusing on cross-disciplinary learning. From these tools, a reinvented timetable structure can emerge.

Meetings are a core system in any organisation. They often fail to engage diverse perspectives unless they are intentionally designed to do so. Rather than working through a linear agenda and looking for majority agreement, tools like 1-2-4-All and What? So What? Now What? are designed to include diverse voices, particularly in groups where conversation might otherwise be dominated by a few. Personal reflection is balanced with structured synthesis, and collective sense-making becomes established as a cultural norm. It enables rapid insight generation, builds psychological safety, and supports a collaborative decision-making culture – essential ingredients for systems that serve people before processes.

The third instalment of Pulse Check helps us to scrutinise how *management and systems* are working for our aspirations for human connection.

Tool 13: Regenerative Ecocycle

Purpose

Help teams assess how time, energy, and resources are currently invested across the school or a specific sub-context, using the ecocycle as a lens for growth, maintenance, renewal, and importantly, letting go. This tool facilitates strategic reflection, identifies bottlenecks or redundancies, and supports conscious decisions about what to evolve, sustain, or stop. The goal is long-term adaptability and regenerative vitality.

Lens

Inspired by biological regeneration and systems thinking, it applies the phases of *birth, maturity, creative destruction,* and *renewal* to initiatives, practices, and routines. Each phase resides in a quadrant that indicates action:

- Analyse
- Decide
- Design
- Grow.

Intended outcomes

- Co-create a visual map to show how energy is distributed across phases of school life
- Gather insight into what is thriving, what is stuck, and what needs to change
- Increase team ownership and strategic clarity about what to evolve, preserve, or disrupt
- A shared understanding of the cycles of growth and renewal within a complex school ecosystem
- Identify areas that are over- or under-resourced
- Build momentum toward continuous adaptation and culturally aligned decision-making.

Materials

Large-format (A1/butcher's paper/newsprint) version of the Regenerative Ecocycle (with the four quadrants); sticky notes; pens. It can also be drawn on a whiteboard.

Credit: Adapted from McCandless and Lipmanowicz (2013).

Process

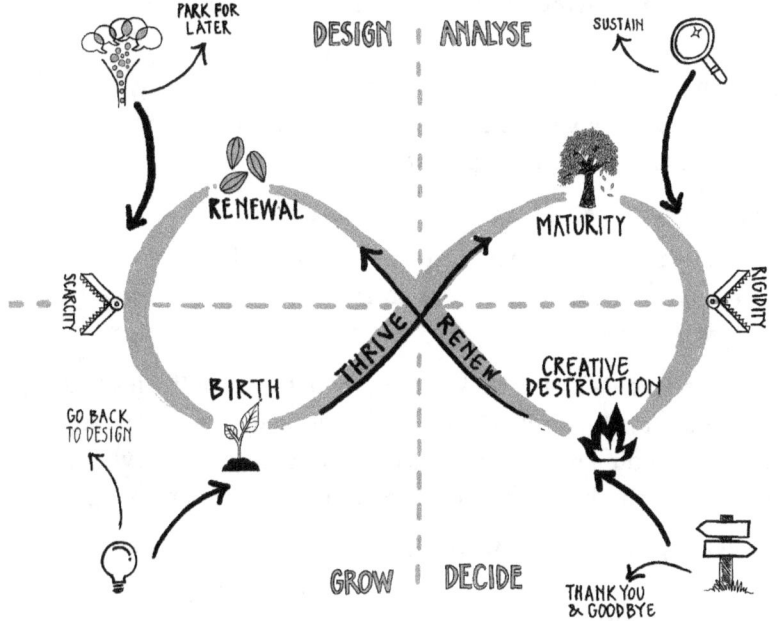

Options:
- Work through the entire process in one setting
- Focus on the quadrants Analyse and Decide, and then return to Design and Grow later.

Gather a team working within the same context (e.g., leadership, middle leaders, faculty team, year level team). Keep groups to a maximum of eight people. Create multiple groups if needed.

Refer to the Explainer below for descriptors of each part of the Regenerative Ecocycle.

1. **Define the scope** – Clarify the focus of your ecocycle mapping.
   Examples:
   - Activities across a school year/term
   - Teaching practices and routines within a subject or grade level
   - Scope of systems currently in place.

2. **Individual reflection** – Within the shared focus, each participant identifies:
   - What is currently occupying our time?
   - What are the activities, routines, or projects consuming energy and resources?

   Write each idea on a separate sticky note. Think broadly, from daily habits (students lining up in the morning) to school-wide programs and events (annual concerts and sports days).

3. **Surface and synthesise** – Without much discussion:
   - Place all sticky notes on a central table or whiteboard.
   - As a group, cluster similar ideas and summarise the emerging themes.

4. **Build the ecocycle** – Using sticky notes, map the key activities to the Maturity quadrant. Ask: What do we routinely keep doing, yet rarely question its ongoing relevance? This might include annual events, timetable and scheduling, and/or behaviour management systems.

5. **Focus on the Analyse and Decide quadrants**

   For each of the emerging themes, identify activities that:
   - Are at Maturity – consuming significant amount of time and resources
   - Are drawing significant resources and belong in the Rigidity Trap
   - Belong in Sustain because they are still relevant and add value
   - Are ready for Creative Destruction
   - Have potential to Renew
   - Are no longer relevant, so you can say, Thank You and Goodbye.

6. **Focus on the Design and Grow quadrants**

   Turn your attention to the activities you identified as having potential to renew. Move activities in Creative Destruction to Renew. For each of these, identify Renewal activities:
   - To be prioritised
   - To Park for Later
   - That are at risk in the Scarcity Trap (the emerging ideas or initiatives that show promise but are lacking the time, support, or resources to thrive).

Apply a design approach to these activities to support their growth. They will give Birth to new initiatives. While some will thrive to Maturity, others may need to Go Back to Design.

7. **Reflect and prioritise**

   Step back and review the map. What does this tell us:
   - Where are we investing too much energy with low return?
   - What needs nurturing or scaling?
   - What are we holding on to that no longer serves us?
   - What is emerging that we need to support or amplify?
   - What are our prioritised design projects?
   - Where do we need to direct our resources (from Rigidity Trap to Scarcity Trap)?

   Identify two or three strategic priorities for immediate next steps or prototyping.

Explainer

- **Sample process:** *Homework is a mature system in school.*

  Have we paused to challenge its ongoing relevance? With emerging Generative AI impact, is homework obsolete in its commonly used form?

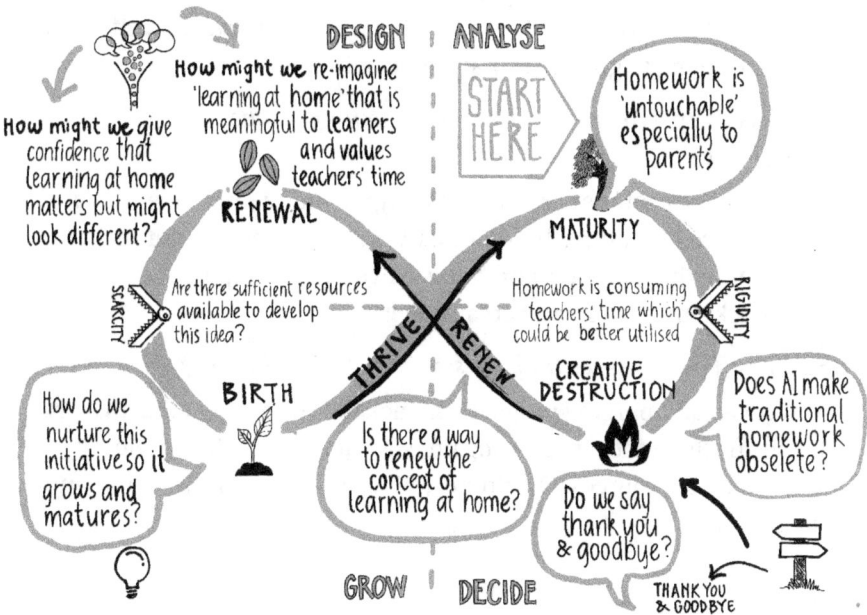

Management and Systems: How We Organise

- **Maturity** – *What are our unexamined assumptions about life at our school?*

    This refers to practices and activities that are established and stable, part of the fabric of school life. These are well-embedded, often efficient, sometimes inefficient, and may be central to how the school functions. However, they must be assessed to ensure they remain aligned with the vision and not simply continued out of habit.

- **Creative Destruction** – *What needs to end, change, or be radically rethought?*

    Which of your mature practices are ready to be intentionally let go or transformed? Some activities may once have served a purpose but are now outdated, misaligned, or draining energy. Creative destruction isn't failure; it's a vital part of renewal and growth.

- **Renewal** – *What are we reinventing or breathing new life into?*

    Which activities in Creative Destruction can be reimagined or refreshed. Renewal requires reflection, design, and the courage to experiment with alternative approaches.

- **Birth** – *What's just beginning? What's full of promise but still fragile?*

    This refers to new ideas, initiatives, or renewed innovations in their early stages. They are often prototypes, emerging from creative thinking, and may still be forming. These activities require nurturing, attention, and resourcing to grow into mature, sustainable practices.

- **Rigidity Trap** – *Are we investing in something just because we always have?*

    This is when resources are overly tied up in mature practices that no longer serve the future. These initiatives may be seen as untouchable, consuming time, energy, and budget, even when impact is limited. This trap blocks innovation and creates inertia.

- **Scarcity Trap** – *Are we under-resourcing the ideas we say we value?*

    New ideas or emerging projects can lack the support needed to thrive. These efforts can feel promising but stall due to insufficient time, attention, or resources. Over time, energy drains, and early momentum is lost.

Tool 14: Breaking Down Silos

Purpose

Disrupt the traditional *paradigm of one*. Create opportunities for teacher collaboration to authentically connect curriculum, and design more integrated, real-world learning experiences. This tool cultivates both pedagogical innovation and organisational coherence by addressing the silos of subjects.

Lens

Cross-disciplinary learning requires deliberate organisational action with system impacts. Schools that prioritise this create the conditions, time, and structures for teachers to work across faculty and beyond grade boundaries. This tool supports strategic curriculum integration and encourages a shift from isolated practice to shared curriculum.

Intended outcomes

- Increase awareness of curricular and capability overlaps across disciplines
- Develop practical plans for cross-disciplinary units or projects that can be piloted and refined
- Create stronger collaborative relationships among staff that model the kind of connected learning we seek for students
- A gradual breakdown of structural silos through co-planning, co-teaching, and shared ownership
- Momentum toward a more agile and interconnected organisational culture.

Materials

Large-format sheets (A1/butcher's paper/newsprint); sticky notes; pens; markers.

Process

Invite faculty/year level groups to work together on cross-disciplinary projects with other faculty/year level groups.

BREAKING DOWN SILOS

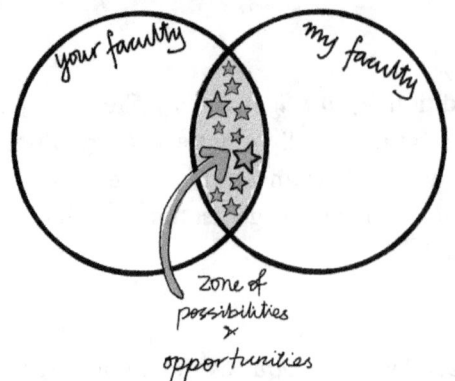

1. **Set the scope**
   - Choose a shared year level or learning project as the anchor for integration.
2. **What is made possible across faculties?**
   - Picture this! What would we like to see?
   - What is our shared vision?
3. **Unpack within faculties**
   - Each faculty team selects a favourite unit or topic, one with potential for a learning project.
   - For this unit, ideate on sticky notes:
     - Key skills/capabilities
     - Student products or outputs
     - Real-world context (refer to Agentic Learning Design).
4. **Cross-pollinate across faculties**
   - Pair up with a different faculty.
   - Find overlaps in content, capabilities, or context.
   - Explore integration opportunities using the Venn diagram to synthesise possibilities and opportunities.
5. **Synthesis and planning**
   - Develop an outline of a joint project or unit.
   - Define shared roles, outputs, and timelines.
6. **Follow up and scale**
   - Have some fun: Use a speed-meeting format to explore more pairings.
   - Plan check-ins to refine and scale successful collaborations.

Tool 15: 1–2–4–All: Purposeful Meetings

Purpose

To redesign meetings by embedding a routine for ideation and decision-making where each voice contributes, and decisions reach a *working consensus*. Structured dialogue allows for collective insight to facilitate inclusivity. It enables each voice to contribute, especially in groups where open discussion often privileges the loudest or most confident group members.

Lens

Meetings represent a highly valuable use of time yet can fail to engage broadly and can feel lacking in purpose. Discussions without structure can allow some voices to dominate while others stay silent. Applying thinking routines as a decision-making process can help lessen these challenges.

Intended outcomes

- High levels of participation and engagement across the group
- Rapid generation and synthesis of diverse ideas and insights
- Increased sense of psychological safety and equity in conversation
- A foundation for actionable next steps or deeper exploration of key themes
- Developing a working consensus.

Materials

Sticky notes; whiteboard or chart paper; pens.

Credit: McCandless & Lipmanowicz (2013).

Process

At each stage:

1. **1 person/1 minute** – Self-reflection: each person silently reflects and writes their response to a prompt
2. **2 people/2 minutes** – With partner: share reflections in pairs and listen for differences or overlap. Group themes.
3. **4 people/4 minutes** – Join another pair to surface common themes and surprises.
4. **All** – Each group shares key insights with the full group. Collate themes for action or deeper exploration.

Tool 16: What? So What? Now What?

Purpose

To structure meaningful reflection that connects observation to insight and action, promoting shared understanding and purposeful next steps.

Lens

By applying abductive reasoning, this reflective dialogue framework shapes the conversation to foster intentional thinking. It supports individual and collective sense-making by guiding participants through three distinct stages: surfacing facts and observations, unpacking meaning, and determining forward action. It is especially useful after a significant experience, as a feedback session or data review.

Intended outcomes

- A shared, accurate picture of what happened and the significance
- Personal and collective meaning-making that invites empathy and deeper understanding
- Concrete next steps grounded in group wisdom
- A culture of learning that values all voices and perspectives.

Materials

Whiteboard or large-format paper divided into three columns labelled *What?* *So What?* and *Now What?*; sticky notes; markers/pens.

Credit: McCandless & Lipmanowicz (2013).

Process

Following a shared experience or workshop session, work through these prompts:

1. **What? (observations and facts)**

    Encourage descriptive, objective thinking:
    - What do we know?
    - What is the pertinent evidence?
    - What happened?
    - What did we see or hear?
    - What are the facts?
    - What more do we need to find out?

    Participants write responses on sticky notes and post them in the first column. Avoid interpretation at this stage; focus on capturing facts, observation, and evidence.

2. **So what? (meaning-making and reflection)**

    Now explore emotional, cognitive and relational resonance:
    - What surprised you?
    - What strikes you about this?
    - Why does this matter?
    - What excites, puzzles, or worries you?
    - How does this make you feel?
    - What do these patterns reveal about our practice, culture or systems?

    Begin with personal reflection, then broaden to group-level insights. Record reflections in the second column.

3. **Now what? (action and commitment)**

    Shift from insight to intent:
    - What do we need to do in response?
    - What might we stop/start/continue?
    - What change is possible, even in a small way?
    - What will it take to shift this?
    - What support or permission is needed?

    Capture next steps and emerging commitments in the third column. These can range from small experiments to longer-term goals.

4. **Debrief and close**
    - Revisit all three columns.
    - Highlight patterns, surprises, and differences.
    - Invite final reflections:
        - What difference will this make?
        - What actions will we take?
    - Assign ownership where appropriate and document action steps.

Pro tip: This framework can be used routinely in team debriefs, reflections, or strategy sessions. Its power lies in creating space for multiple perspectives and building a bridge from thought to action.

Tool 17: Pulse Check: Management and Systems

Purpose

To evaluate and improve the current operational aspects by surfacing what's working well, and where improvements are needed. This reflective activity provides a structured, empathic approach to examining the school experience through the lens of not only the efficiency of the systems but also their effectiveness in supporting the vision for learner experience and an aligned professional culture.

Lens

A future-focused school intentionally monitors the management and systems in place to remain responsive, relevant, and inclusive. This tool brings a critical eye to the present by asking: *Are we effectively prioritising the human connection elements?* It invites a cycle of continuous improvement that values both affirmation and honest critique.

Intended outcomes

- Determine if current systems are effectively enabling or constraining future-focused vision and professional culture
- Identify operational inefficiencies or areas of duplication
- Plan improvements to enhance agility, clarity, and responsiveness.

Materials

Print or draw Management and Systems: What's Working Well? and Even Better if..., as shown below, on large-format sheets (A2 or A3/butcher's paper/newsprint); markers; pens; sticky notes.

Process

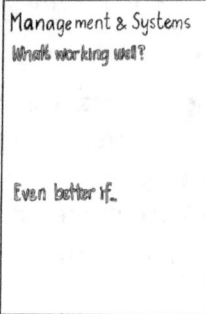

1. **Frame the activity** – Introduce the goal of the session: to evaluate how current management structures and operational systems align with the school's vision and support the desired professional culture. You may use this to focus on one particular area as the lens through which to consider the responses.

   The activity is best when undertaken in groups of four to five, with responses then aggregated.

2. **Affirm: What's working well?** Invite participants to reflect on and respond to current operational practices that support your school's vision and desired culture.

   Prompt examples:
   - What areas show promise and add value?
   - How is the human connection supported by the management and systems?

3. **Challenge: Even Better If…** Now turn to areas for growth. Encourage participants to name what is misaligned, missing, or could be strengthened to better serve the vision and culture.

   Prompt examples:
   - What systems feel outdated, confusing, or unnecessary?
   - Where are the barriers and obstacles to human connection?
   - What are potential opportunities for improvement?

4. **Thematic synthesis** – As a team, group sticky notes into themes. Use subheadings or categories (e.g., classroom culture, assessment, transitions, student voice) to clarify key areas of focus.

Look for:
- Repetition or resonance across responses
- Differences between staff perspectives and student insights
- Personas that are under-supported or over-represented.

5. **Prioritise and plan** – Identify two or three high-impact opportunities for immediate or short-term action. For each, consider:
   - What small shift could we implement now?
   - Who will lead the next step or prototype a solution?
   - How will we follow up or evaluate change?
   - Consider a deeper dive using the Regenerative Ecocycle to explore further.

Chapter 11

Places, Spaces, and Resources: What We Create

A transforming school is not only built on relationships and operational systems, but is also shaped by its physical environment and the material resources it provides. Every space sends a message about the activity that occurs there, who it is for, and how they are valued. When deliberately designed, the spaces around us can elevate our values and reinforce culture, scaffolding the systems we aim to grow. But when overlooked or disconnected, even the most beautifully constructed spaces can unintentionally reinforce unaligned practices. In this section, we examine how to align the physical and material landscape with your school's aspirations so that every place, space, and material resource becomes an expression of purpose and possibility.

School transformation occurs when *learner experience* reflects a shared vision for the future, *professional culture* is cohesive and aligned, *management and systems* support growth, and *places, spaces, and resources* are purposefully designed so that people are empowered to learn, work, and thrive together.

Why this matters

Learning spaces are not merely passive backdrops to our important work. They are the vehicle that can actively shape interactions, nurture engagement, and support learning. Physical environments can be the tangible enablers of the vision and culture we hope to see. While we all know creative and inspiring teachers can engage and motivate students anywhere, how much more effective could it be if learning spaces were intentionally designed to align with the strategic vision of a transforming school? While spaces might be the *front* stage, effectiveness requires deep thinking and significant *backstage* work, to create the environment where everyone can thrive, learning and working at their best.

In the past, accommodating the physical classroom has been driven by efficiency and maximising scale:

- How many students?
- How many square metres per student?
- How many classrooms?
- How many desks?
- How many chairs?
- Where is the front?

While purchasing efficiencies and prudent resourcing are not to be ignored, the specifications can work with aspirations for *learner experience* and the complementary *professional culture*. Decisions of places, spaces, and resources begin with understanding the vision, and how this creates our aspirations for human connection in the learning environment. All of this impacts the 'what' of the learning environment – *What we create*.

Once we have clarity of the human connection elements and supporting systems, we can turn our attention to the spatial design and fit-out that might enable this. Here's what I've found: the provision of space alone will not transform learning. I have shared the consequences of spatial design and fit-out that occur without a complementary strategy to transform culture (*how we will work*). Let's not pretend that the *Field of Dreams* principle ('if you build it, they will come') applies, because the reality is, if you (decide to) build it, there is significant work to be done (before, during, and after).

An essential ingredient that is seemingly missing in pre-service and in-service teacher education is the idea of growing teachers' spatial literacy. In-person learning occurs within a physical environment, and each is different. Unless tables are bolted to the floor, then we are able to move the furniture and play with different configurations that can enhance the learner experience. Amplifying spatial literacy gives teachers the confidence to adapt, adjust, and play with the space.

I am naturally wired to feel space and to understand how people use it and make adjustments along the way. As a young teacher, I regularly rearranged the classroom; my goals were to maximise empty floor space or provide better opportunities for different ways of organising the learning. There were times when I would notice that something wasn't quite right, so I would tweak a few things. At other times I would completely rearrange. All this within a normal-size (and even smaller) classroom: imagine if it was designed with these affordances in mind?

Enhancing spatial literacy is to increase understanding and application of space as the 'third teacher'. The idea emerged powerfully in the book *The Third Teacher: 79 Ways You Can Use Design to Transform Teaching and Learning*. This seminal work by Bruce Mau Design and collaborators in 2010 reframed the learning environment as an active agent in shaping learner behaviour, engagement, and wellbeing. Drawing inspiration from Reggio and Montessori philosophies,, they challenged us to see every physical element – light, layout, materials, visibility, flexibility – as a pedagogical choice. It encouraged schools to disrupt traditional spatial norms and ask bold questions:

- Does this space invite curiosity?
- Does it support collaboration?
- Is it adaptable to diverse learners?

The goal was to empower us to rethink not just *what* happens in school, but *where* and *how* it happens, reinforcing that space itself plays a part in transforming the learning and social experience in your community.

The Third Teacher presented 79 ways to transform learning and teaching – and the first one?

> **#1 Everyone can be a designer** – Look to many sources for design inspiration.

I spend time with educators, visiting schools with contemporary design, helping them to adopt the mindset of a designer, to step out of their own school, to be curious, observant, and open to opportunities. I help to unpack the challenges, rather than leap to the solution ('We just need sofas and coffee tables'). I encourage the reframing: *What problem are we seeking to solve?*

But we don't stop there. The mindset of a designer seeks to absorb insight from different places, beyond our familiar milieu, where people work, learn, play, socialise, gather, and recharge. Together, we not only look to schools, but also libraries, museums, co-working spaces, playgrounds, hotel lobbies, airport lounges, and cafés. And, as Bruce Mau and colleagues wrote:

> **#16. Emulate Museums** – An environment rich in evocative objects... triggers active learning by letting students pick what to engage with.

How can we emulate museums if we haven't visited them recently and observed the activity through the eyes of the learner? This domain, *places, spaces, and resources*, requires a designer mindset, building on all the thinking up to this point.

From human connection to design principles

Reflecting on the preceding elements, each contributed to the spatial design considerations. We began with:

Learner experience – Who are we designing for?

Professional culture – How will we work?

Empathy mapping and journey mapping activities apply to both learner and professional perspectives and help understand the 'users', their problems and needs to thrive and flourish. Looking Back Across Generations and Three Horizons Thinking helped to unpack future perspectives that matter.

With these outcomes in mind, we considered:

Management and systems – How will we organise?

The implications from the human connection impact how we manage time and resources. Allowing for deeper and cross-disciplinary learning asks, *What is made possible?* This encourages both collaborative practice and thinking about the connections between subjects. Such projects will have impacts on timetables and scheduling, staffing, and resourcing.

All of this affects the physical and material elements. This is critical as we turn attention to:

Places, spaces, and resources – What will we create?

We can begin by co-creating design principles that articulate what matters most in a learning environment. This is before any furniture is chosen or floorplans are drawn. These principles act as a compass, guiding small and large decisions in the design process so that the physical space aligns with the school's vision, pedagogy, and culture. Rather than starting with aesthetics or logistics, we begin with purpose.

For example, a school might adopt principles such as:

- Spaces support learner agency and collaboration.
- Flexibility is essential to support varied teaching and learning modes.
- Design will foster belonging, safety, and visibility.
- Spaces will feel welcoming and calming.

The design principles can translate educational and wellbeing values into spatial intent, ensuring that the resulting environments actively support articulated aspirations. In this way, design becomes strategic, not just functional or decorative.

Each of the practical action workshops that follow build on the work that has gone before by providing clarity on design principles that reinforce vision, growing spatial literacy for the complementary professional practice, and supporting you to design the physical and material elements for your school to transform.

Tool 18: Amplifying Spatial Literacy

Purpose

To build awareness of how space influences behaviour, engagement, and interaction, both intentionally and unintentionally. This activity facilitates a deeper understanding of spatial dynamics and provides tools to design learning environments that align with pedagogy and purpose.

Lens

Spaces speak. The physical environment acts as a third teacher, shaping how learning unfolds. Yet, we often work in inherited spaces that don't reflect our desired practice or what we value for the future. This activity draws on everyday spatial experiences to explore how principles of comfort, flow, and intentionality can inform more purposeful learning design.

If you are in a building process, this workshop would be a helpful preparation for the teachers who will be working in the new space.

Intended outcomes

- Create alignment in co-teaching teams
- Increased awareness of spatial design on a positive learning community
- Development of shared principles about the learning environment
- A tangible artefact reflecting a reimagined learning environment
- Growing spatial literacy among teams, shifting from inherited space to intentional design
- A practical bridge between pedagogy and place, anchoring learning environments in lived user experience.

Materials

Large-format sheets (A2 or A3/butcher's paper/newsprint); sticky notes; pens; markers.

Resources

- Appendix 1: Setting the Scene – Café or Classroom
- Appendix 2: Café Design Principles Explained
- Appendix 3: Bubble Drawings.

Process

Work in teams that regularly share a space or work in proximity.

This workshop can be:

- Held at school as reflective and practical dialogue (Option 1), or
- As field ethnographers, collecting insights through observation (Option 2).

Option 1: Theoretical and reflective (at school)

1. **Stimulus story**
    - Share the Coles Cafeteria story (Appendix 1).
    - Prompt: What's your favourite café and why?

2. **Collaborative research**

    Read the café design principles (Appendix 2):
    - Intuitive layout and flow
    - Comfortable and varied seating
    - Thoughtful lighting and acoustics
    - Aesthetic appeal and branding
    - Ergonomic design for staff
    - Natural elements to soften and humanise the space.

3. **Group discussion**
    - Why do these design principles matter to our café experience as users?
    - Why do these design principles matter to the staff and their responsibilities?
    - Do these insights translate to enhanced learning space design?

    Transition into parallels with learning environment design questions:
    - How do learners choose where and how to work?
    - What does our current spatial layout signal about how learning occurs?
    - What matters the most to us about the spaces around us?
    - What will our students need from school to flourish in the future?

4. **Output options**
    - Use What? So What? Now What? to unpack insights and develop ideas/actions (p. 148).
    - Create bubble drawings (see Appendix 4) to create 'Our Dream Space'.
    - Co-create a set of design principles for your learning space.

Option 2: Field ethnographers (off-site)

1. **Visit a café, library, co-working and/or informal learning/gathering space**
   - Observe how people use space: where they connect, how they move, where they linger.
   - Record findings through photos, sketches, or notes (maintain privacy/ask for permission).

2. **Explore café design principles**
   - Intuitive layout and flow
   - Comfortable and varied seating
   - Thoughtful lighting and acoustics
   - Aesthetic appeal and branding
   - Ergonomic design for staff.

   (See Appendix 2: Café Design Principles Explained.)

3. **Reconvene to share insights and relate them to your school context**

   Record responses to each question (sticky notes or on a shared doc).
   - Why do these design principles matter to our café experience as users?
   - Why do these design principles matter to the staff and their responsibilities?
   - Do these insights translate to enhanced learning space design?

   Transition into parallels with learning environment design questions.
   - How do learners choose where and how to work?
   - What does our current spatial layout signal about how learning occurs?
   - What matters the most to us about the spaces around us?
   - What will our students need from school to flourish in the future?

4. **Output options**
   - Use What? So What? Now What? to unpack insights and develop ideas/actions (p. 148).
   - Create bubble drawings (see Appendix 4) to create 'Our Dream Space'.
   - Co-create a set of Spatial Design Principles for your learning space.

Tool 19: Spatial Design Principles

Purpose

To articulate a set of shared design principles that will guide future spatial planning, creating alignment with educational vision, values, and learner needs.

Lens

For a new project, the collaborative development of design principles guides the design process. When we define what matters most before working with design professionals, we enter the partnership with clarity, shared language, and confidence. These principles become a touchstone, helping schools to advocate for spaces that support learning, rather than adapting learning to suit the space.

The educators and learners who inhabit an existing learning space can also establish their design principles to maintain alignment of the physical and material elements with vision and purpose, for learning and social connection.

Intended outcomes

You will leave this process with a co-created, contextualised, and values-driven set of design principles. These will serve as both a touchstone and a filter, helping you stay aligned with your educational purpose so that your spaces truly become the third teacher.

Materials

Each section that follows includes the specific resources needed.

Process

1. **The current reality**
   - Take a walk-and-talk audit of school spaces.
   - Record What's Working Well ? / Even Better If…
   - Collate responses into key insights.

2. **Our core beliefs**
   - Revisit your school vision and values.

- Ask: What do we believe about optimal conditions for *learner experience* and *professional practice*?
- Record responses on large sheets, then summarise key spatial implications.

3. **Translate beliefs into reality – Our Dream School**
    - Use *pedagogical typologies* (Appendix 3) to assess current versus desired teaching approaches:
        - Teacher-led
        - Teacher-supported
        - Teacher-initiated.

Pie chart #1: Create a pie chart to show *current* learner experience.

Discussion: Pedagogy and design – What do learners need to thrive?
- Explore integration of pedagogy with physical design.
- Provoke thinking through future learning trends and analysis.

Pie chart #2: Create a pie chart to show desired learner experience.

(This activity is also included in Designing for Future Learner Experience.)

- Explore *spatial typologies* (Appendix 3): classrooms, commons, outdoor zones, etc. Discuss:
    - What would we like to include?
    - How would we use each area?
- Develop bubble drawings to visualise ideal learning environments (Appendix 4).

4. **Co-create design responses**
    - Rotate groups of two to four people through prompts (5 minutes on each):
        - Our spaces will… (relate to vision/learner experience aspirations)
        - We value places that… (relate to values and mission)
        - Learning environments must… (relate to learner experience and professional culture)
        - Social spaces matter because…
        - Outdoor areas can…
        - Movement needs to be…
        - The aesthetic must reflect…

- The future is evident through...

5. **Synthesise**
   - Allocate a pair to each set of prompts to identify themes.
   - Report back to the group.
   - Synthesise responses into five to seven clear, aspirational, and actionable principles.

Please note: For a larger-scale project (masterplan, new building), the process of co-creating design responses can engage a broader cross-section of the community and the synthesis can be undertaken by the project team.

For a smaller scale (a shared teaching space), the team can include the students in creating design responses and then work through the synthesis together.

6. **Reflection and feedback**
   - Test principles against existing spaces.
   - Share with the wider community for feedback, ensuring alignment with school vision

Tool 20: Affordances A–Z

Purpose

To build spatial literacy by exploring the concept of affordances (opportunities a space enables or invites) and applying these to the design of purposeful, responsive learning environments. This hands-on activity connects pedagogical intentions to physical aspects that support them.

It could follow the Amplifying Spatial Literacy and Spatial Design Principles activities to apply the ideas and insights.

Lens

Spaces communicate values, and each design decision impacts emotions and behaviour. Drawing from spatial typologies and learning affordances, this activity invites you to think like learning designers, planning not only what happens in a space, but what the space itself enables. This activity grows collaborative, creative thinking around the design of inclusive and flexible environments.

Intended outcomes

- Shared language around spatial affordances
- Prototype learning spaces designed for multiple uses
- Increased creative collaboration among educators
- Creative fun.

Materials

Printed A-Z Affordance Cards (Appendix 5); large-format paper; craft supplies; markers; glue sticks; large paper.

What are affordances? See the Explainer below.

Process

For each group: Print and cut out a set of Affordance Cards for each group and bundle them together face down or in a bag (see Appendix: 5: A-Z Affordance Cards).

1. **Your affordances**
   - Each team draws four random cards.

- Discuss what each affordance enables and how it applies to learning, emotions, and behaviours.

2. **Trade and choose**
   - Option to trade two cards with another group or swap out two cards from your pile (no peeking).

3. **Design team collaborative conversation**
   - Articulate your vision for the space
   - Focus: year level/subject/s

4. **Design and build**
   - Create a visual model of a space that integrates all four affordances using craft materials or drawing.
   - Consider layout, lighting, zoning, flow, sensory factors, and engagement.

5. **Gallery walk**
   - Share designs with other teams.

6. **Reflection**
   - Teams explain how each affordance is addressed in their plan.
   - Encourage reflection:
     - What assumptions about space were challenged?
     - How creative did you get?
     - Which affordances feel under-represented in your current environment?

Explainer

But first: What are affordances?

Affordances refer to the qualities or features of an object, space, or environment that suggest how it can be used. Originally coined by psychologist James J. Gibson (2015) in relation to objects, it was later expanded more broadly into design contexts. Applying the term 'affordances' helps us understand how people intuitively interact with their surroundings in intended and unintended ways. For example, while:

- A chair affords sitting, it is also used as a step-up to reach a higher shelf
- A handle affords pulling, it is also used for hanging items to dry
- Wide-open spaces afford large group gatherings, they are also used for quiet contemplation.

In physical environments, affordances also include subtle cues, lighting, layout, acoustics, or flexibility, which invite or inhibit certain behaviours such as collaboration, focus, play, or reflection.

Understanding affordances is foundational to spatial literacy. When we design or use learning spaces intentionally, we're not just re-arranging furniture, but shaping how students might feel, behave, and engage. A space with movable furniture may afford group work, while a quiet nook with soft lighting might afford reading and calm. Recognising and designing for affordances helps schools move beyond one-size-fits-all layouts and instead create environments that are responsive, inclusive, and aligned with their learning values.

Tool 21: Designing for Future Learner Experience

Purpose

To explore the alignment between learning experience, space, and transforming schools for the future. Through site visits, reflection, and synthesis, this session helps us to begin shaping a vision for learning environments grounded in student needs and future-focused pedagogy.

Lens

Transformation begins with understanding both the current context and the opportunities the future might bring. This session bridges observational learning through personal experience and visits to other places, with analysis of pedagogical and spatial practices, using the student experience pie chart (from Amplifying Spatial Literacy) as a guide.

Intended outcomes

- Clarity on the current pedagogical landscape and aspirations for the future
- A shared language for discussing learning spatial typologies
- Initial alignment between pedagogy, space, and student needs
- Executive-level commitment to the human-centred transformation journey.

Materials

Printed Spatial and Pedagogical Typologies (Appendix 3); sticky notes; large sheets; pens.

Process

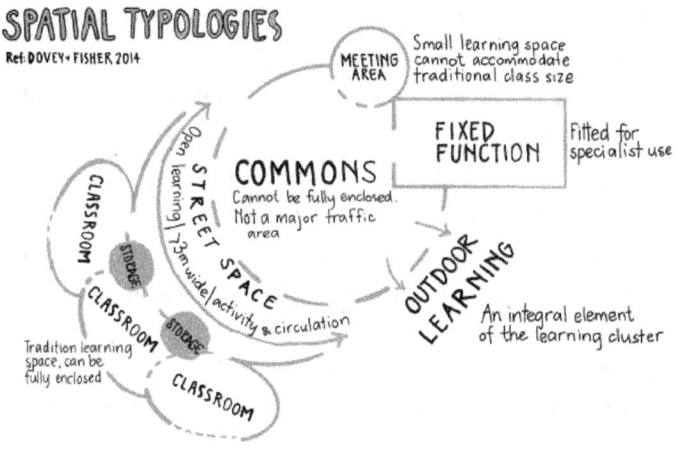

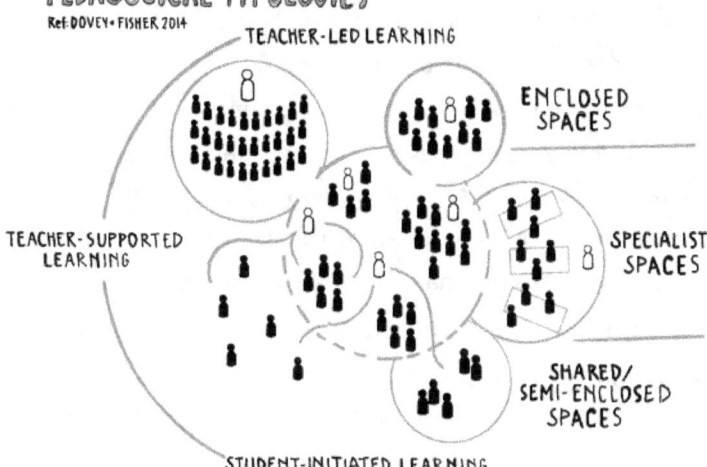

Groups of four to six participants.

1. **Introduction and context**
   - Brief overview of intent, context, and the importance of re-imagining design.
   - Desirable: Organise site visits to other schools, tertiary settings, and workplace environments.

   Alternatively: Observe the use of different areas around your school.
   - Synthesise key insights from site visits.

- Unpack thoughts, reflections and ideas using the Spatial Typologies and Pedagogical Typologies artefacts by applying What? So What? Now What?
- Identify aspirational elements that could inform school design.

2. **Context analysis**

   Analyse/discuss current practices that represent student experience (see Pedagogical Typologies):
   - **Teacher-led learning** – The teacher directs the learning process, setting goals, content, and tasks to be completed, with students following structured guidance.
   - **Teacher-supported learning** – The teacher scaffolds learning experiences, offering guidance while deliberately enabling students to build autonomy as learners.
   - **Student-initiated learning** – Students take the lead in setting learning goals and direction, with the teacher acting as a mentor or resource to support agentic inquiry.

   Review previous discussion of the artefacts.

   Pie chart #1. Create a pie chart to show current learner experience.

   Discussion: Pedagogy and design – What do learners need to thrive?
   - Explore integration of pedagogy with physical design.
   - Provoke thinking through future learning trends and analysis

   Pie chart #2. Create a pie chart to show *desired* learner experience.

   (You may have already completed this in Spatial Design Principles.)

3. **Spatial typology analysis**

   Examine how the use of different spatial types aligns with the *desired* learner experience.

   On Spatial Typologies, use sticky notes to identify opportunities and challenges in each space shown. Assess the relevance and suitability of the spatial types for the future learner experience: classrooms, commons, street spaces, fixed-function rooms, meeting areas, outdoor zones, and storage. Prepare a presentation to share with the other groups.

4. **Wrap-up**
   - Consolidate thinking and reflect on the human element of transformation. Share discussion and reflection.
   - Synthesis: What? So What? Now What? (p. 148).

Tool 22: Pulse Check: Places, Spaces, and Resources

Purpose

To evaluate the physical and material environment in supporting learning, culture, and the systems and structures.

Lens

Reflect on the spatial affordances (or limitations) in current learning, communal spaces, both indoor and outdoor.

Intended outcomes

- Understand how space enables or constrains teaching and learning
- Identify underutilised or misaligned spaces
- Plan adjustments to align environments with pedagogical intentions.

Materials

Printed or drawn Places, Spaces, and Resources: What's Working Well? and Even Better if..., as shown below, on large-format sheets (A2 or A3/butcher's paper/newsprint); markers; pens; sticky notes.

Process

Facilitate a session with your team, take a walk around the school, then reflect on your observations:

1. **What's working well?** Affirm aspects of *places, spaces, and resources* that support the vision for *learner experience*, the aspirations for *professional culture*, and how we organise our *management and systems*.

2. **Even better if...** Critique those aspects that are unaligned and suggest areas where *places, spaces, and resources* might be enhanced.

   Synthesise the responses into key themes.

   Prioritise next steps based on highest-impact areas.

Final Word
It Starts with Trust

> 'Progress means not just changing
> but changing for the better.'
>
> – C. S. Lewis

When I began my PhD journey in 2016, I could not have imagined how profoundly both the world and I would change. Writing through the upheaval of the COVID-19 pandemic in 2020 and 2021, I found myself navigating a period marked by complexity, disruption, and transformation. It was, for all of us, a time of re-evaluation. In those months of lockdown, uncertainty, and remote-everything, the questions I was asking about education became deeply personal. I wasn't just studying change and complexity; I was living it.

This is a field guide to rethinking learning environments for the future. It is about space and pedagogy, about collaboration and systems, about empowering learners and enabling teachers. But like all good design, it became iterative. As I wrote, reflected, and worked with school communities across different contexts, it became clear that what we are really trying to change is not a room or a roster, but a relational and cultural ecosystem. This is the real terrain of transformation.

Across the chapters of this book, I have shared insights on learner experience, organisational design, physical environments, and the all-important professional culture of schools. I have highlighted the shift from rigid models of schooling to more adaptive, fluid approaches, designing for learner agency. The tools and practices outlined here are drawn from real teachers and leadership teams willing to try something different. But even the most exciting and innovative ideas fall flat without one essential ingredient: *trust*.

Why trust matters more than ever

Trust is often spoken about in vague or sentimental terms, yet its presence (or absence) is a measurable force in any organisation. During the pandemic, we saw how schools with deep reservoirs of trust were often more agile in responding to crisis. Educators had to redesign everything overnight. Those who succeeded did not necessarily have the best tech, the most detailed plans, or a head start on hybrid learning. They succeeded because there was trust.

Trust is what enables non-hierarchical leadership. It's what allows someone to suggest a crazy idea that messes with convention or have the courage to break from the problem-fix loop. It's what gives students a voice and a sense of belonging. It's what allows us to question the familiar routines we've always accepted as unchangeable. When trust is present, people feel safe to explore, to fail forward, and to lead.

But not all trust is created equal. Bryk and Schneider (2002) identify three types of trust in schools:

- **Organic trust**, based on position or moral authority: 'They're the principal, so I trust them.'
- **Contractual trust**, built on agreements and mutual expectations: 'I'll do my part if you do yours.'
- **Relational trust**, the richest and most sustainable: 'I trust you because you've shown care, competence, and consistency.'

Relational trust is the kind that fuels transformation. It cannot be mandated. It grows slowly, through shared work, honesty, and time. It underpins successful transformation, whether it's restructuring a timetable, reimagining student agency, or redesigning a vision-led physical space.

The journey of the book

This book has followed a conceptual arc, beginning with the big ideas that emerged from my thesis. It then moved into practical action as we explored the four elements:

1. **Learner experience** – Grounded in empathy and purpose. Where learners are people to be known, grown, and empowered.
2. **Professional culture** – Defined by purpose, people, and trust. The living and breathing cultural norms of a school either amplify or suppress innovation and progress.

3. **Management and systems** – The invisible architecture of a school. How we design timetables, teams, and roles; how we allocate resources in alignment with our vision and values.
4. **Places, spaces, and resources** – Not just space as backdrop, but space as pedagogical tool, *the third teacher*.

At the centre of each of these elements is **a belief in people**. Change and making progress toward a preferred future will not be achieved by creating workable structures alone, but by building capacity, culture, and courage. The concept of a field guide is deliberately not a map with directions, but a toolkit for navigating your own terrain. There is no one path, but there are common patterns, pitfalls, and possibilities.

Practising what we preach

Throughout, I've advocated for a design mindset: observing deeply, listening well, prototyping boldly. But these actions are not merely technical; they are also relational. Who we are in the process of change matters just as much as what we change, which returns to trust.

Leaders set the tone. When leaders show they trust their staff by listening, by being transparent, by authentic presence, and by acknowledging uncertainty, they create a culture where others can also trust. This culture ripples outwards: to teams, to students and beyond. It becomes safe to ask questions, to challenge norms, to grow.

Building trust is not always comfortable. In fact, it's often uncomfortable. But discomfort is a sign of learning. As I was writing my thesis in the depths of the pandemic, I realised I was being reshaped too, becoming more open to messiness, more determined to disrupt the status quo, and more willing to sit with uncertainty. These are the emotional dimensions of transformation we must acknowledge.

A future-facing hope

I don't believe we should aim to 'get back to normal'. Ever. Normal was never designed with every learner in mind. Instead, we must move forward and embrace complexity with courage, creativity, and compassion. The future is not some far-off destination we prepare students for. It shapes how we engage with them, now.

And yet, none of this is possible without trust.

Trust is the thread that weaves through everything in this book, every framework, every strategy, every conversation. Without it, transformation falters. With it, transformation takes root.

So, as you close this book, I invite you to pause and consider your next step.

Whether you're a principal, a teacher-leader, or a system-level strategist, ask yourself:

- Who do I trust?
- Who trusts me?
- What will I do tomorrow to grow that trust?

Because transformation doesn't begin with a new timetable, or policy, or architectural plan.

It begins with a relationship.

A conversation.

A shared commitment to change for the better.

It begins, and it endures, with trust.

Appendix 1
Setting the Scene – Café or Classroom

Today's cafés are intentionally designed to support different experiences – areas for focus, connection, or collaboration. School spaces increasingly serve similar diverse purposes. The shift from cafeteria to café reflects a cultural move away from efficiency towards human experience. Likewise, learning space design is evolving, where standardised classrooms give way to adaptable environments that reflect the varied ways people learn and connect. Making this shift requires a shared language about space, grounded in co-constructed design principles.

Living in Sydney, where coffee culture runs deep, my family shares a long-standing appreciation for good coffee. Even though we can make excellent coffee at home, we still go to cafés. Why? Because a café is about more than just the coffee (and muffins!).

Before we talk cafés, let's go back to the Coles Cafeteria of my youth. In the 1970s, a trip to the city was a major outing, dressed in our 'best' of course. There was always a stop at the ubiquitous cafeteria – it was a highlight. But the space was purely functional: queues, trays, rapid turnover. It was loud, hard-surfaced, and impersonal, designed for the staff to efficiently go about their work, not for connection.

By the 1980s, cafeterias were in decline, replaced by a growing café culture. While franchised cafes became common, many of us preferred the intimacy of locally owned cafés. The clinical design of cafeterias shifted to bespoke and diverse layouts. Efficiency was replaced by ambience: the hum of conversation, music in the background, the smell of fresh coffee, a chat with the barista, and spaces that welcomed people to pause and connect.

This made me think about schools. When I enter a café, I choose my seat based on my purpose, and the best cafés offer options:

- A cosy corner with armchairs for reading or quiet conversation

- A communal table for group connection or shared moments
- A high stool at the window for focused solo time
- A lively table amid the buzz for social connection.

The decline of the cafeteria shows us what people now value: intentional, human-centred design, rather than the efficiency of the in-and-out cafeteria. Similarly, school design has moved away from one-size-fits-all. Instead, we're designing spaces that adapt to pedagogical needs, and social connection. After all, great learning occurs in a social context.

To do this well, we need *spatial literacy*, an understanding of how design influences behaviour, learning, and interaction. When we develop this literacy, we gain the skills to evaluate, reimagine, and design learning spaces with purpose.

Appendix 2
Café Design Principles Explained

Intuitive layout and flow: A well-designed café guides customers seamlessly from entry to ordering to seating. Clear pathways and logical progression reduce confusion and make the space feel more comfortable.

Comfortable and varied seating: Offering a mix of seating options, such as cosy corners, communal tables, and bar seating, shows an understanding of diverse customer preferences.

Thoughtful lighting: Balancing natural and artificial lighting creates a warm ambience. Soft, indirect lighting reduces glare and fosters a relaxed environment, while brighter task lighting ensures functionality where needed.

Efficient queuing system: Designing an ordering area that is intuitive and spacious prevents congestion and enhances the customer experience. Clear signage and designated waiting zones contribute to a smoother flow.

Aesthetic appeal and branding: Incorporating unique design elements, such as artwork or distinctive furniture, perhaps creating Instagrammable moments, reinforces the café's brand identity and attracts customers.

Barista-friendly workspace: Designing an efficient, ergonomic workspace for baristas ensures quick service and maintains a clean, organised appearance, contributing to the overall customer experience.

Acoustic considerations: Incorporating materials that absorb sound can reduce noise levels, making conversations more enjoyable and the environment more pleasant.

Natural elements: Introducing plants or natural materials can enhance the ambience, making the space feel more inviting and comfortable.

(From https://www.boardandvellum.com/blog/elements-of-great-cafe-design/)

Appendix 3
Spatial and Pedagogical Typologies

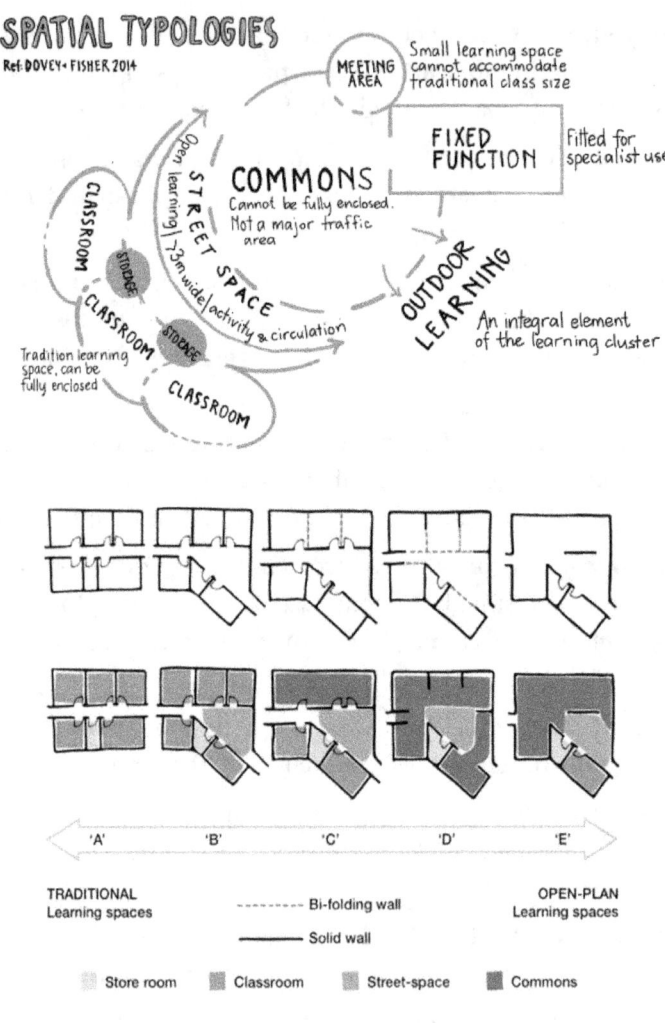

Learning space types (adapted by Imms et al., 2016)

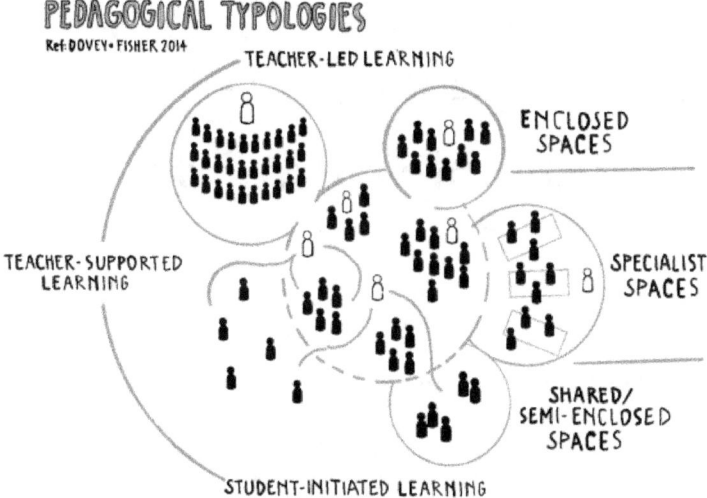

Teacher-led learning: The teacher directs the learning process, setting goals, content, and tasks to be completed, with students following structured guidance.

Teacher-supported learning: The teacher scaffolds learning experiences, offering guidance while deliberately enabling students to build autonomy as learners.

Student-initiated learning: Students take the lead in setting learning goals and direction, with the teacher acting as a mentor or resource to support agentic inquiry.

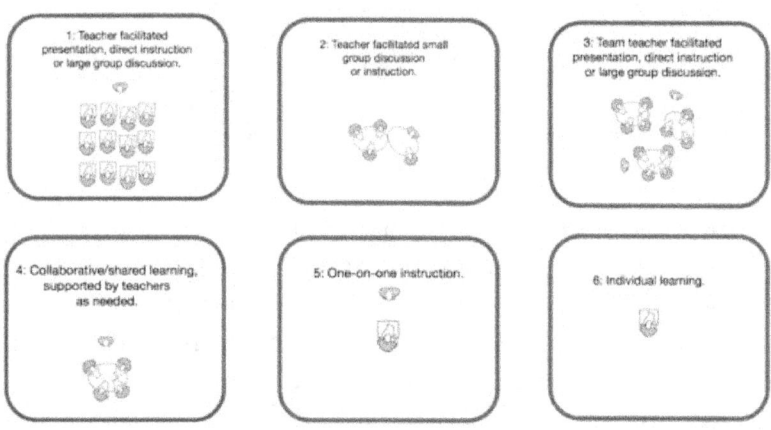

Dovey and Fisher's (2014) learning space types, as adapted in Imms, Cleveland, and Fisher (2016)

Appendix 4
Bubble Drawings

What are bubble drawings and how are they used?

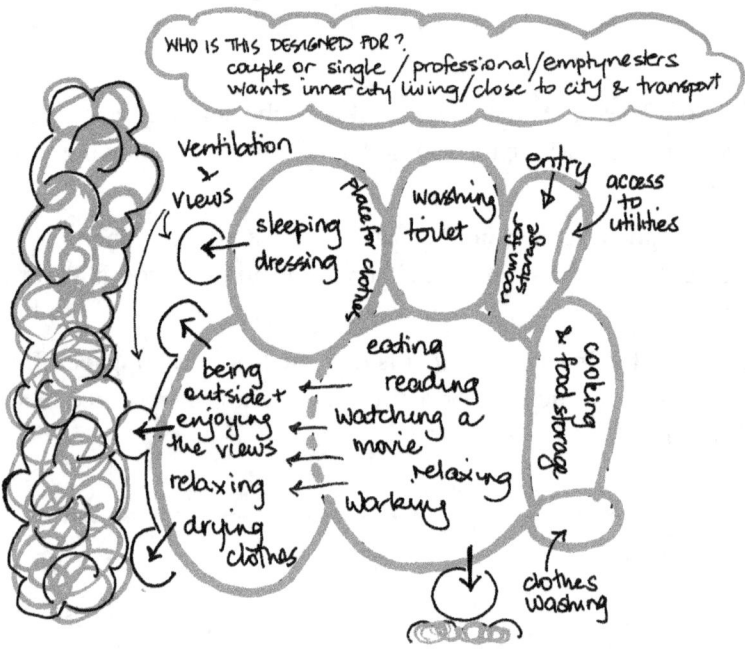

In the early stages of a design project, before any walls are drawn or specifications decided, architects use bubble drawings as a quick, visual, and shared process to show spatial relationships and test ideas. These sketches use loose, hand-drawn 'bubbles' to represent key functional zones or activities and the connections between spaces without locking in dimensions, structure, or detail.

Rather than focusing on form or finishings, bubble diagrams ask:
- What spaces do we need?
- How should these spaces relate to each other?
- Which areas need strong connections or alignments? Which need separation?
- Where are the flows of movement and energy?

The bubbles are deliberately messy and iterative, often drawn on tracing paper and adjusted in real-time during conversations with clients and colleagues.

Bubble drawings are especially useful in educational settings because they make space planning accessible and collaborative, to engage in meaningful co-design conversations. They help teams identify early opportunities and constraints, surfacing issues with noise, visibility, or movement, well before plans are fixed. Most importantly, bubble drawings reinforce the principle that function should drive form; where the purpose of each space guides its layout, ensuring the design serves learning rather than forcing learning to adapt to the design.

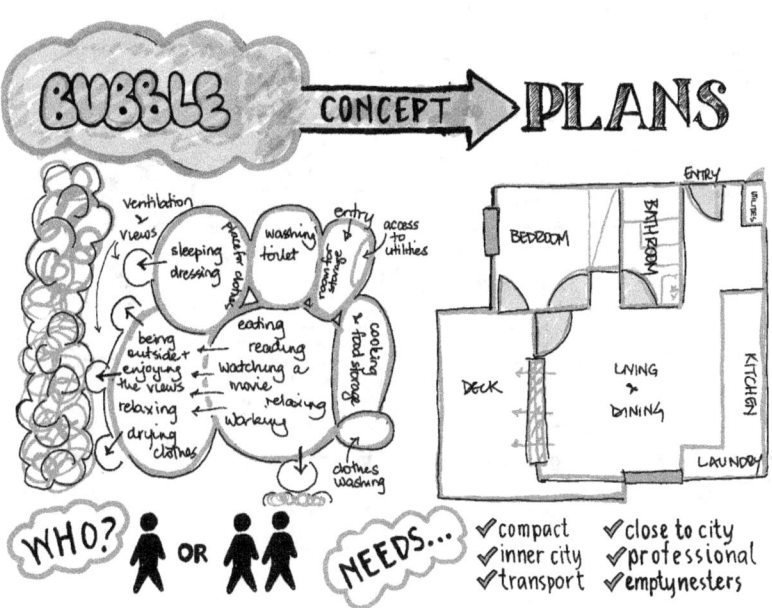

Appendix 5
A-Z Affordance Cards

Active
promote movement, hands-on, and physical activity.

Biophilic
integrate natural elements to enhance well-being and cognitive function.

Collaborative
support team projects, discussion, and co-construction of knowledge.

Direct teaching
Instruction and focused attention, for clarity and cognition.

Embodied
not just hands-on, but 'body-on' learning.

Feedback
opportunity for a conversation, scrutinising progress and next steps.

Group rotations
station-based learning, peer engagement, and differentiated instruction.

Hive
dynamic, multi-use hub for social learning, collective problem-solving, and creative collaboration.

Immersive
transport learners into deeply engaging, multi-sensory and thematic experiences.

Junction
transition zones that connect learning zones, fostering serendipitous moments.

Kinetic
encourage movement, active exploration, and physical engagement with learning.

Loud
high energy, using instruments and equipment.

Maker
hands-on, creative spaces where learners experiment, prototype, and bring ideas to life.

Nurturing
for emotional well-being, belonging, and psychological safety.

Outside
extend beyond the internal space, leveraging nature and open environments.

Play
support exploration, social connection, and the power of unstructured learning.

Quiet
dedicated to focus, deep thinking, and independent work.

Reflective
encourage metacognition, self-assessment, and thoughtful processing.

Sensory
support diverse learning needs through varied textures, lighting, with acoustic considerations.

Tech-infused
multi-media devices and apps to augment learning.

Understanding
deeper learning in small groups or one-on-one.

Versatile
multiple uses/no fixed function.

Welcoming
inviting environments that foster inclusivity, safety, and a sense of belonging.

eXperimental
exploring, hypothesising and testing ideas. Hands-on, showing curiosity.

Yarning
circular spaces designed for storytelling, dialogue, and cultural knowledge-sharing.

Zoning
strategic design of learning areas that delineate different modes of learning and interaction.

References

Anderson, J., & Winthrop, R. (2025). *The disengaged teen: Helping kids learn better, live better and feel better*. Penguin Random House.

Biggs, J. (1988). Approaches to the enhancement of tertiary teaching. *Higher Education Research and Development, 7*(1).

Board & Vellum. (n.d.). *Elements of great cafe design*. https://www.boardandvellum.com/blog/elements-of-great-cafe-design/

Brown, B. (2018). *Dare to lead: Brave work. Tough conversations. Whole hearts.* Random House.

Bryk, A. S., & Schneider, B. L. (2002). *Trust in schools: A core resource for improvement*. Russell Sage Foundation.

Critchlow, H. (2019). *Joined-up thinking: The science of collective intelligence and its power to change our lives*. Hodder & Stoughton.

Dovey, K., & Fisher, K. (2014). Designing for adaptation: The school as socio-spatial assemblage. *Journal of Architecture, 19*(1), 43-63.

Gibson, J. J. (2015). *The ecological approach to visual perception*. Psychology Press.

Gislason, N. (2010). Architectural design and the learning environment: A framework for school design research. *Learning Environments Research, 13*(2), 127-45.

Goffman, E. (1959). *The presentation of self in everyday life*. Doubleday.

Goodwin, K. (2020, April 29). *Kate Raworth's Three Horizons Framework intro - a guide for workshop use. Medium*. https://matchboxstudio.medium.com/kate-raworths-three-horizons-framework-intro-a-guide-for-workshop-use-5e25235c587d

Harari, Y. N. (2018). *21 lessons for the 21st century*. Spiegel & Grau.

Hattie, J. A. C., & Donoghue, G. M. (2016). Learning strategies: A synthesis and conceptual model. *NPJ Science of Learning, 1*, 16013.

Hattie, J., & Zierer, K. (2018). *10 mindframes for visible learning: Teaching for success*. Routledge.

Hutchins, E. (1995). *Cognition in the wild*. MIT Press.

Imms, W., & Byers, T. (2016). Innovative learning environments: Facilitating change to 21st-century teaching and learning. *LEaRN Technical Reports*, University of Melbourne.

Imms, W., Cleveland, B., & Fisher, K. (2016). *Evaluating learning environments: Snapshots of emerging issues, methods and knowledge*. Sense Publishers.

Knock, A. (2022). *The beauty of a complex future: Redefining teacher success and sustainability in innovative learning environments* [Doctoral dissertation, University of Melbourne]. Minerva Access.

Lackney, J. A. (2008). Teacher environmental competence in elementary school environments. *Children, Youth and Environments, 18*(2), 133-59.

Lawson, B. R. (2006). *How designers think - The design process demystified*. Routledge.

Marton, F., & Säljö, R. (1976). On qualitative differences in learning: I – Outcome and process. *British Journal of Educational Psychology, 46*(1), 4-11.

McCandless, K., & Lipmanowicz, H. (2013). *The surprising power of liberating structures: Simple rules to unleash a culture of innovation.* Liberating Structures Press.

Murphy Paul, A. (2021). *The extended mind: The power of thinking outside the brain.* Houghton Mifflin Harcourt.

PEP Worldwide. (2019). *Personal efficiency program: Create conditions to allow you to work best* [Unpublished training manual]. PEP Worldwide.

PWP/P Architects, VS Furniture, & Bruce Mau Design. (2010). *The third teacher: 79 ways you can use design to transform teaching and learning.* Abrams.

Senge, P. M. (1990). *The fifth discipline: The art and practice of the learning organization.* Doubleday.

Schein, E. (2009). *The corporate culture survival guide* (New and revised edition). Jossey-Bass.

Sharpe, B. (2013). *Three horizons: The patterning of hope.* Triarchy Press.

Sinek, S. (2011). *Start with why: How great leaders inspire everyone to take action.* Portfolio.

Snowden, D. J., & Boone, M. E. (2007, November). A leader's framework for decision making. *Harvard Business Review.*

Thornburg, D. D. (2004). Campfires in cyberspace: Primordial metaphors for learning in the 21st century. *International Journal of Instructional Technology and Distance Learning, 1*(10), 3-10.

Timperley, H. (2008). Teacher professional learning and development. *Educational Practices Series, 18.*

Willis, K. (2024). *Good nature: The new science of how nature improves our health.* Bloomsbury Publishing.

Wright, N. (2017). Disrupting the 'paradigm of one': Restructuring structures to integrate learning in a modern learning environment. *Journal of Educational Leadership, Policy and Practice, 32*(1), 48-61.

www.ingramcontent.com/pod-product-compliance
Lightning Source LLC
Chambersburg PA
CBHW052029070526
44584CB00016B/1968